BON JO

(these Days)

Wise Publications
London / New York / Sydney / Copenhagen / Madrid

Exclusive Distributors:

Music Sales Limited
8/9 Frith Street,
London W1V 5TZ, England.

Music Sales Pty Limited
120 Rothschild Avenue,
Rosebery, NSW 2018, Australia.

Order No. AM933251
ISBN 0-7119-5267-1
This book © Copyright 1995 by Wise Publications.

Music arranged by Arthur Dick.
Music processed by Paul Ewers Music Design.

Your Guarantee of Quality:

As publishers, we strive to produce every book to the highest commercial standards.

Whilst endeavouring to retain the original running order of the recorded album,
the book has been carefully designed to minimise awkward page turns and to
make playing from it a real pleasure.

Particular care has been given to specifying acid-free, neutral-sized paper made from
pulps which have not been elemental chlorine bleached. This pulp is from farmed sustainable
forests and was produced with special regard for the environment.

Throughout, the printing and binding have been planned to ensure a sturdy,
attractive publication which should give years of enjoyment.

If your copy fails to meet our high standards, please inform us and we will gladly replace it.

Music Sales' complete catalogue describes thousands of titles and
is available in full colour sections by subject, direct from Music Sales Limited.
Please state your areas of interest and send a cheque/postal order for £1.50 for postage to:
Music Sales Limited, Newmarket Road, Bury St. Edmunds, Suffolk IP33 3YB.

Printed in the United Kingdom

Hey God

Words & Music by Jon Bon Jovi & Richie Sambora

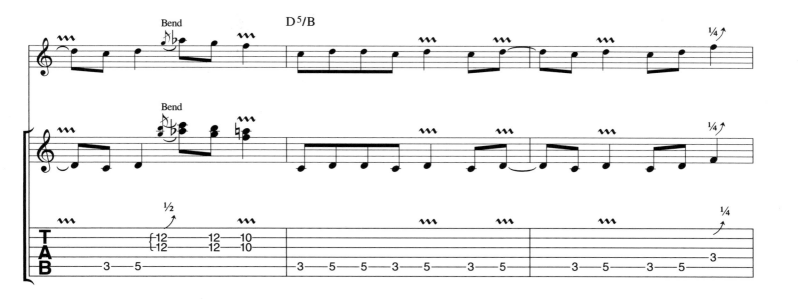

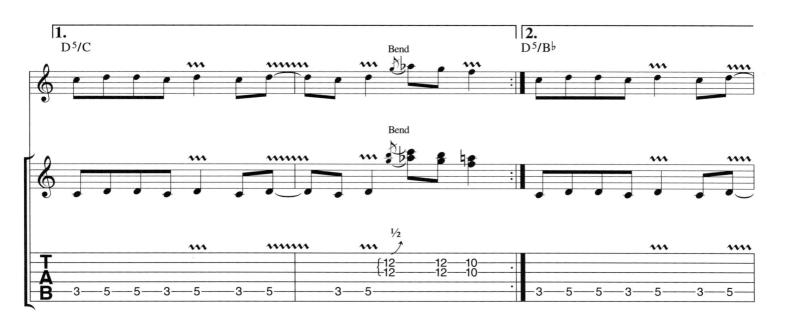

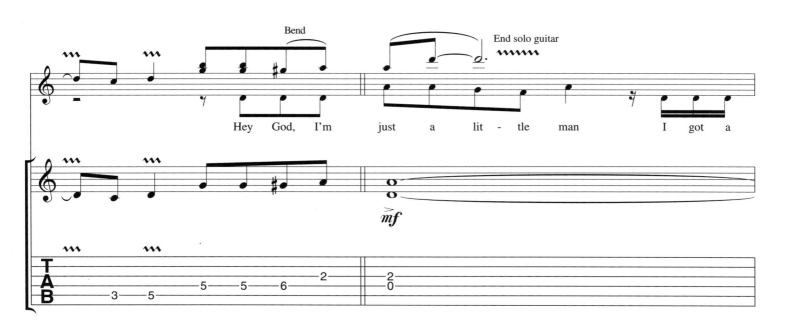

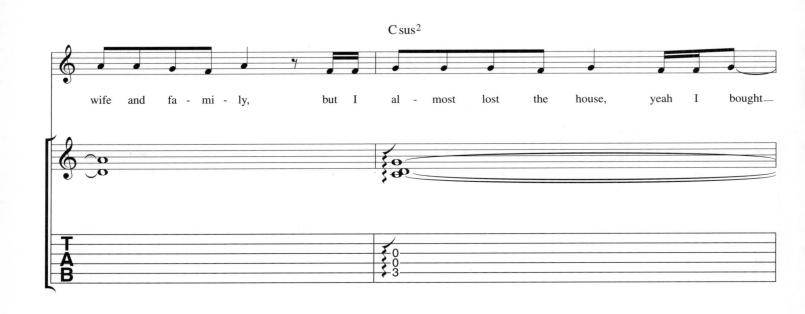

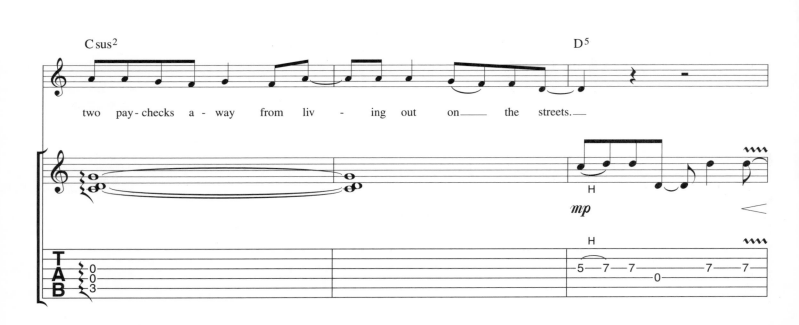

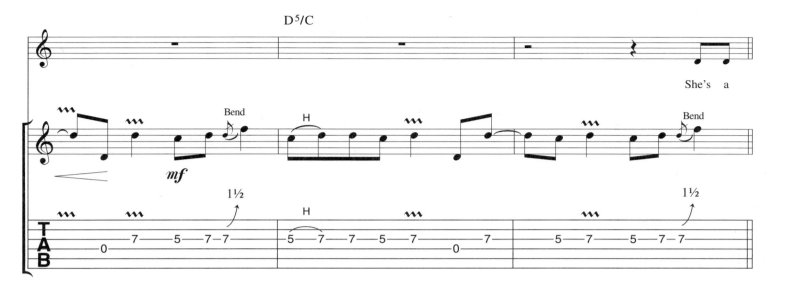

D⁵/C

She's a

VERSE

D⁵

work - ing sin - gle mum, like a saint she don't com - plain, she
(Verse 2 see block lyric)

Let ring... *sim.*

*Arrangement of Dan Electro coral sitar accompaniment

D⁵/C

nev - er says a word but she thinks—— that she's to blame,—— her

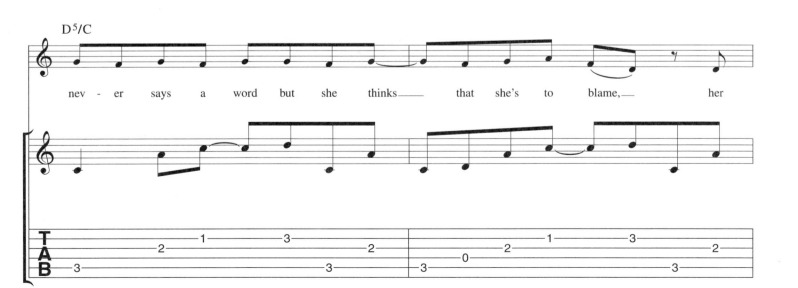

son just got con - vic - ted, he blew some cop a - way, she

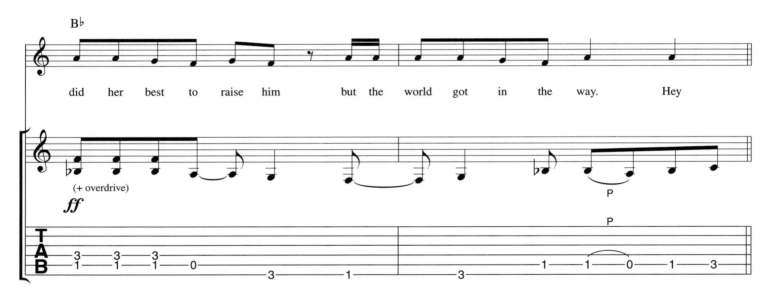

did her best to raise him but the world got in the way. Hey

CHORUS

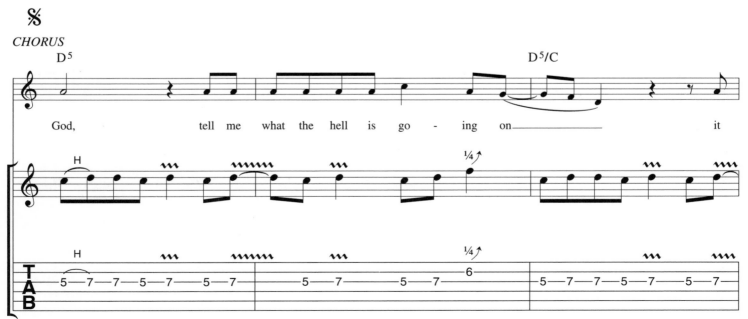

God, tell me what the hell is go - ing on _____ it

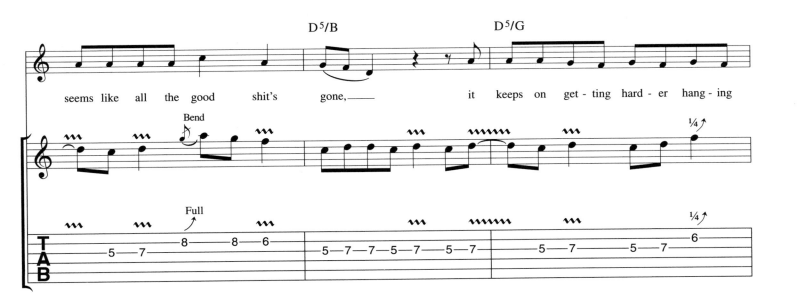

seems like all the good shit's gone,_____ it keeps on get - ting hard - er hang - ing

on,_____ but hey, hey, hey, hey, God, there's

nights you know I want to scream,_____ these days you're ev - en hard - er to be -

11

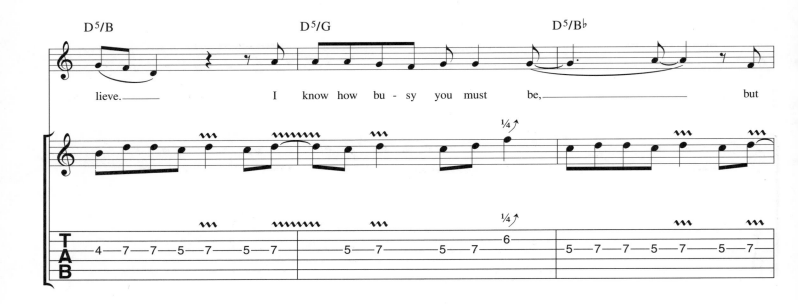

lieve._____ I know how bu - sy you must be,_____ but

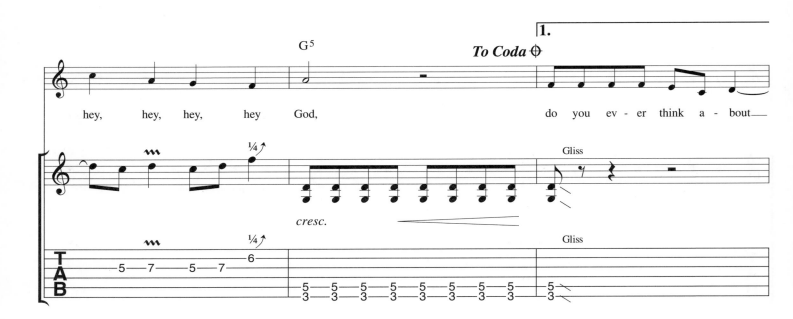

hey, hey, hey, hey God, do you ev - er think a - bout____

_____ me?

*Dan Electro coral sitar

do   you   ev - er   think   a - bout_____   me?

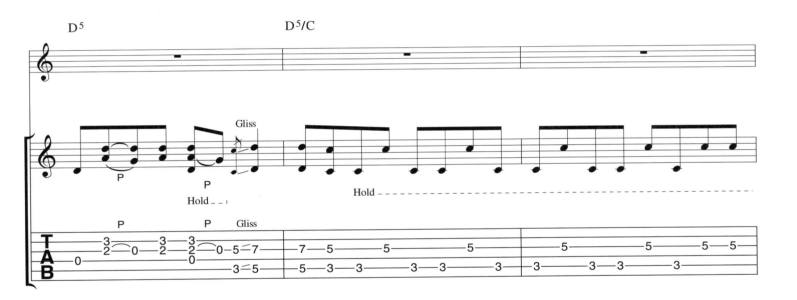

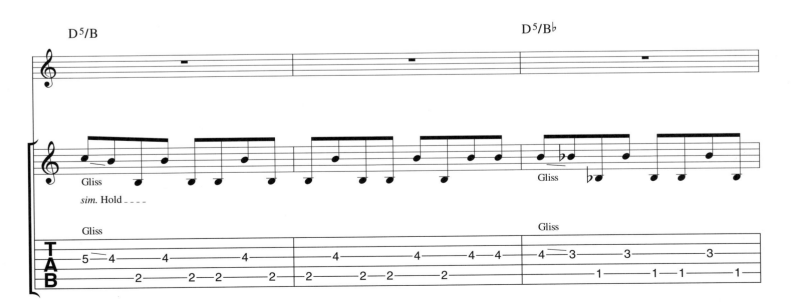

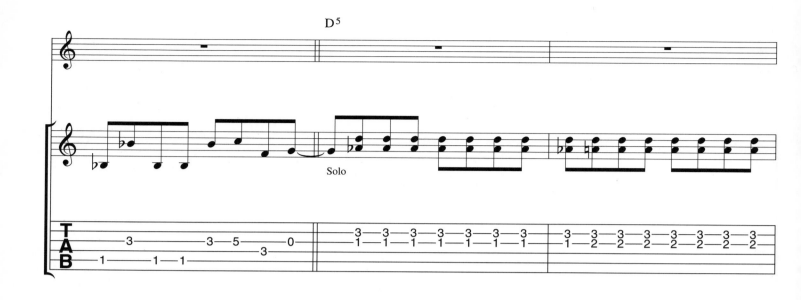

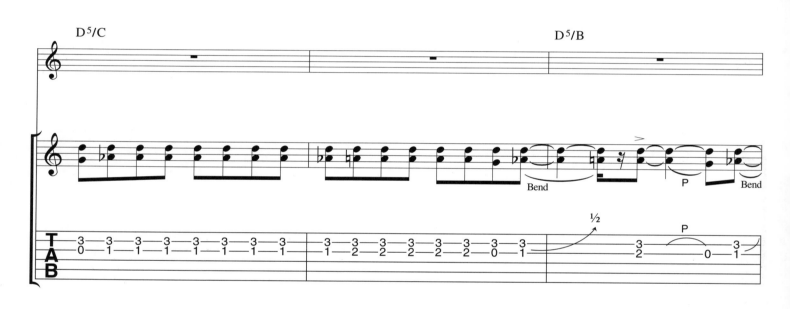

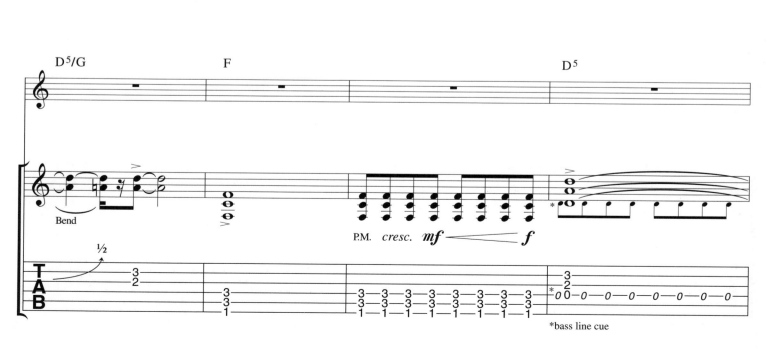

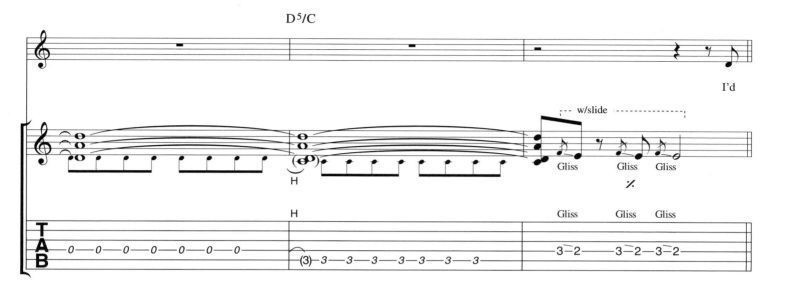

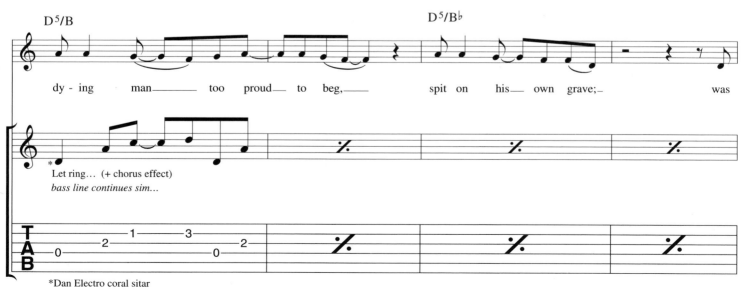

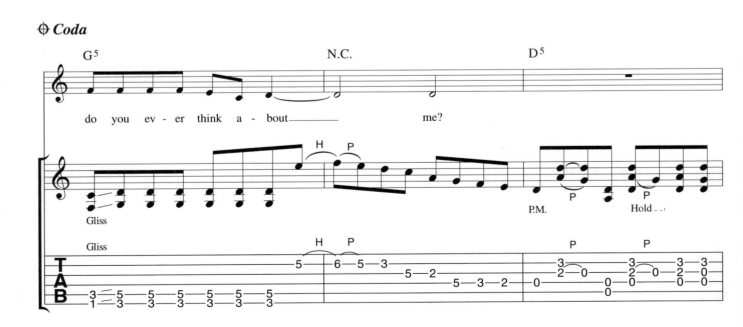

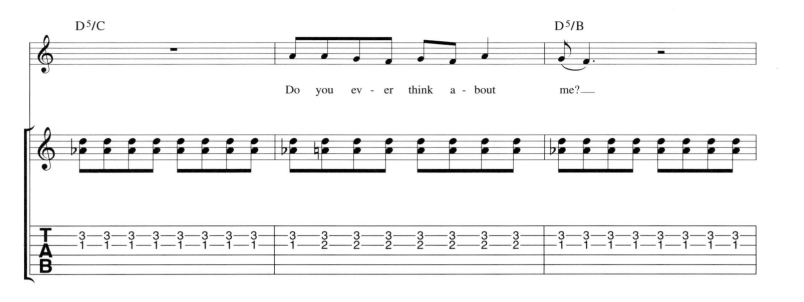

Do you ev-er think a-bout me?

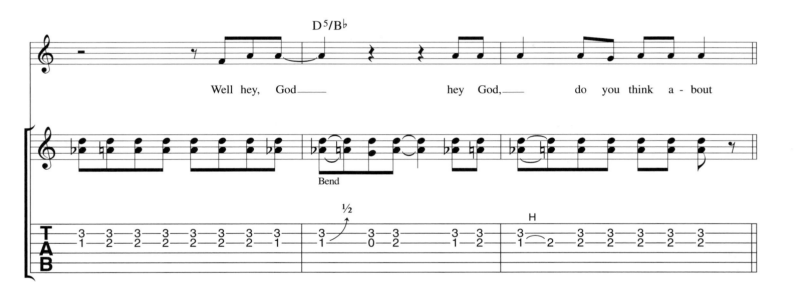

Well hey, God____ hey God,____ do you think a-bout

Vocals ad lib.

me?

Gliss
Strum

sim.

Gliss

⊓ = downstroke   ∨ = upstroke

Do you ev-er think a-bout me?___ Hey God,

hey God, hey God, do you think a-bout

*Play 3 times
with ad lib.
guitar solo*

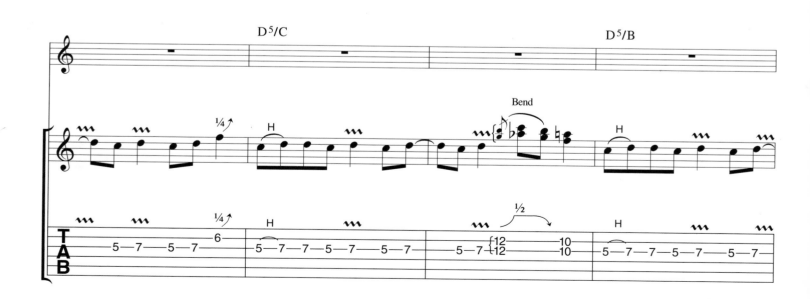

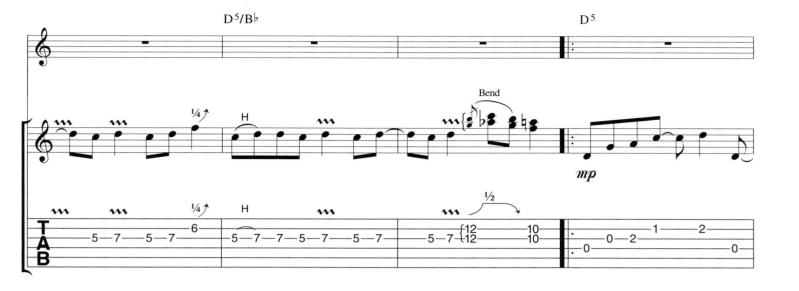

Verse 2:
Born into the ghetto in nineteen ninety-one
Just a happy child playing beneath the summer sun
A vacant lot's his playground, by twelve he's got a gun
The odds are bet against him, junior don't make twenty-one.

Something For The Pain

Words & Music by Jon Bon Jovi, Richie Sambora & Desmond Child

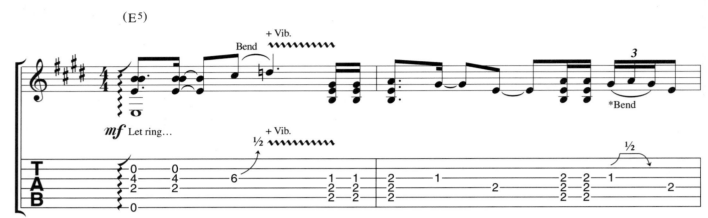

This is an arrangement of the Dan Electro coral sitar   *Bend is flat

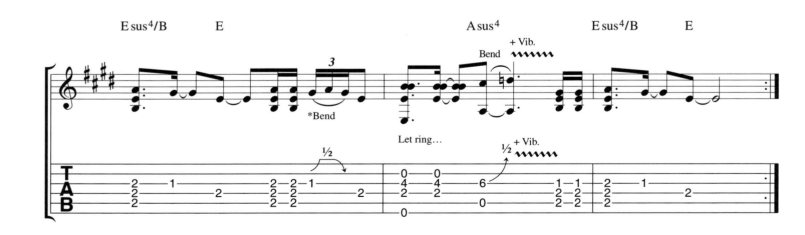

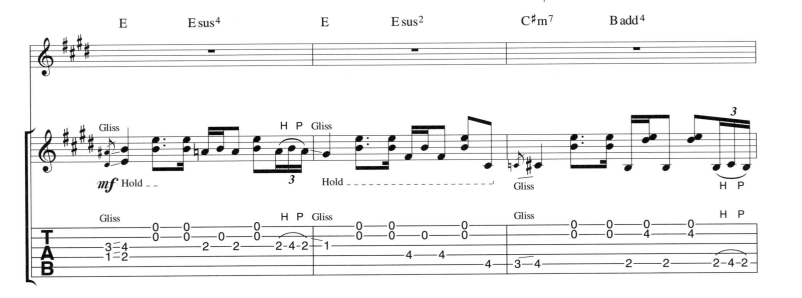

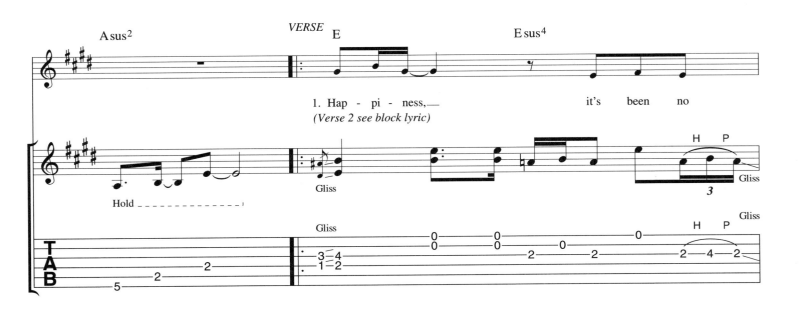

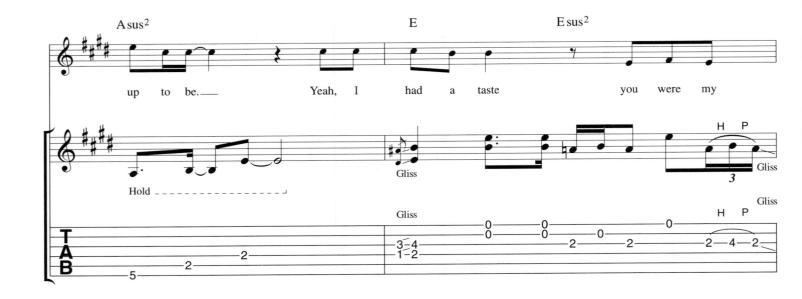

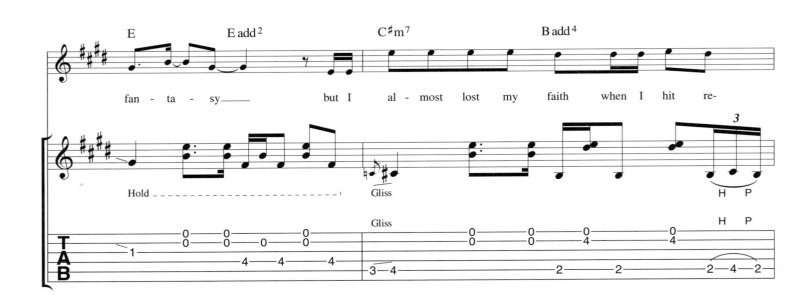

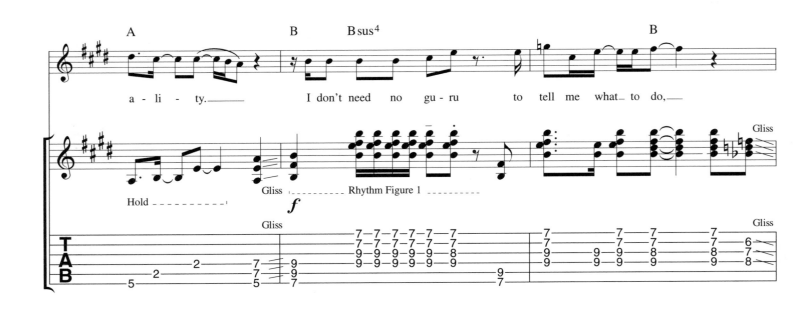

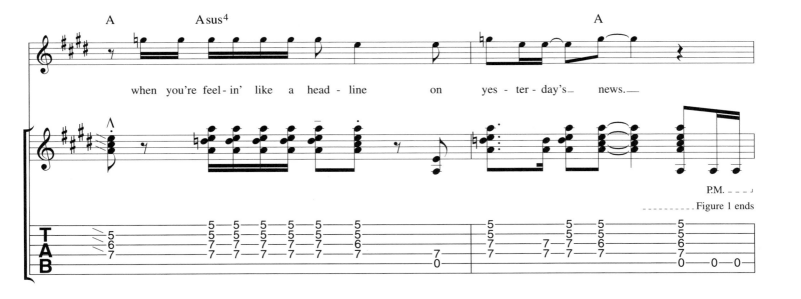

when you're feel-in' like a head-line on yes-ter-day's news.

P.M.
Figure 1 ends

CHORUS

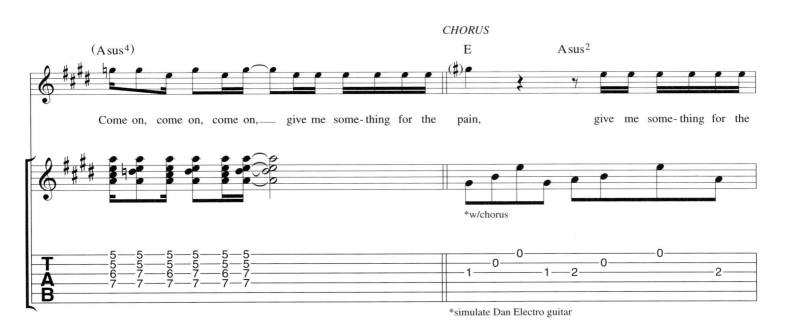

Come on, come on, come on,— give me some-thing for the pain, give me some-thing for the

*w/chorus

*simulate Dan Electro guitar

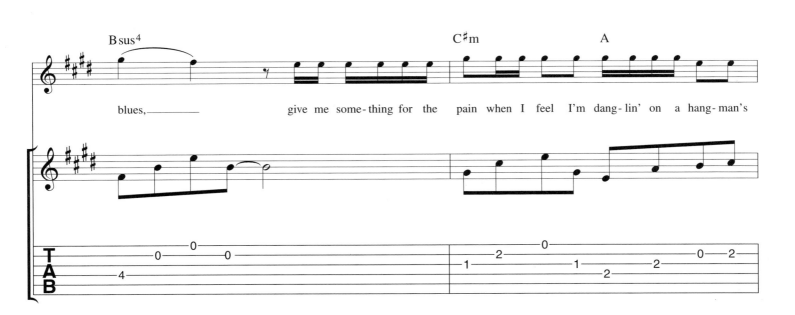

blues,— give me some-thing for the pain when I feel I'm dang-lin' on a hang-man's

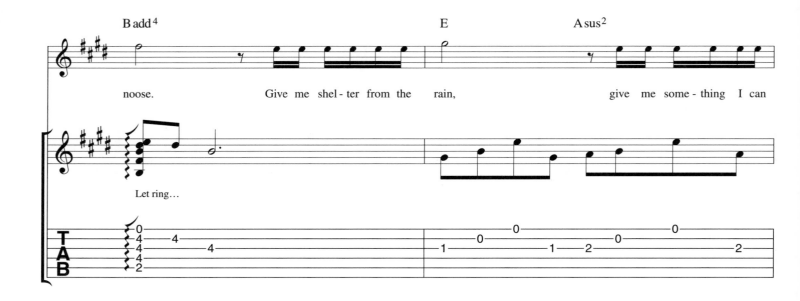

noose. Give me shel - ter from the rain, give me some - thing I can

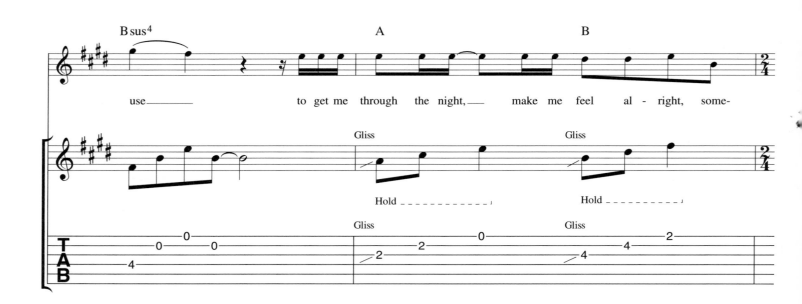

use to get me through the night, make me feel al - right, some-

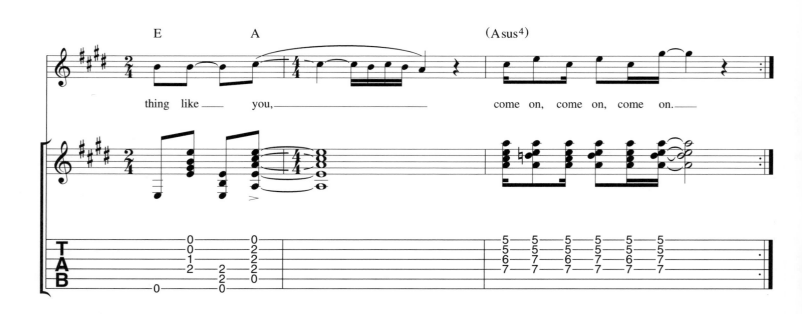

thing like you, come on, come on, come on.

Solo
With Rhythm Figure 1

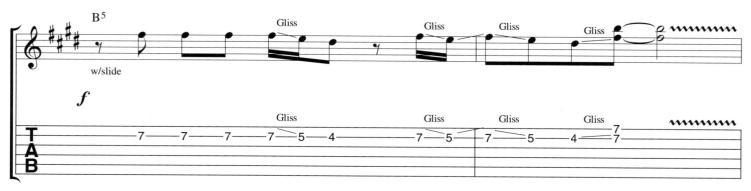

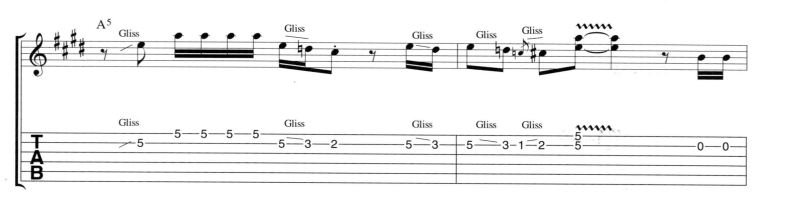

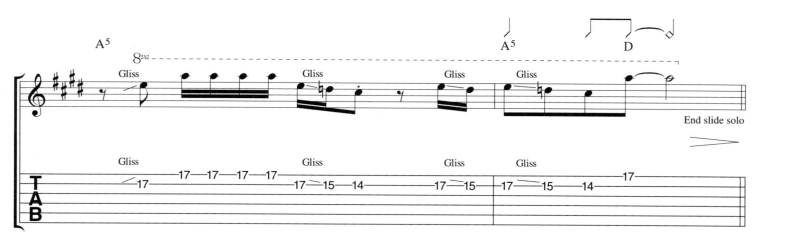

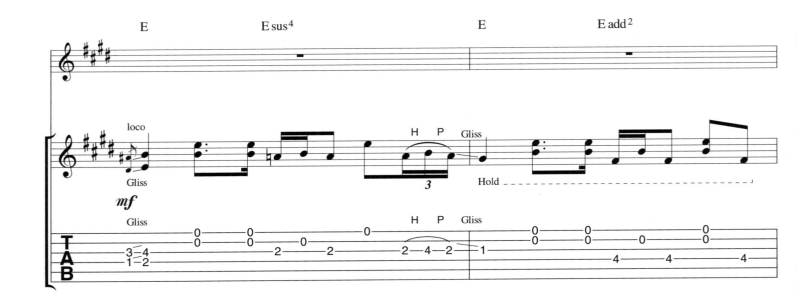

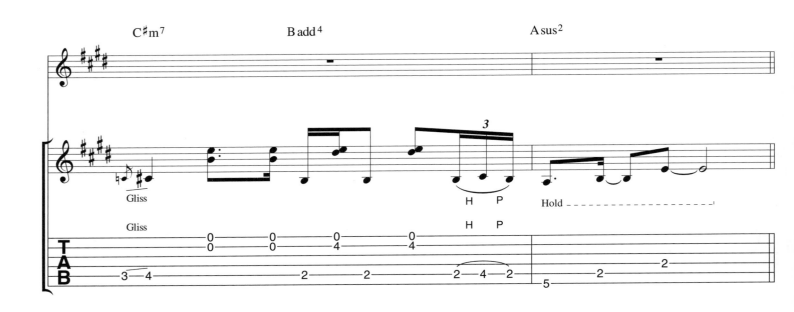

VERSE

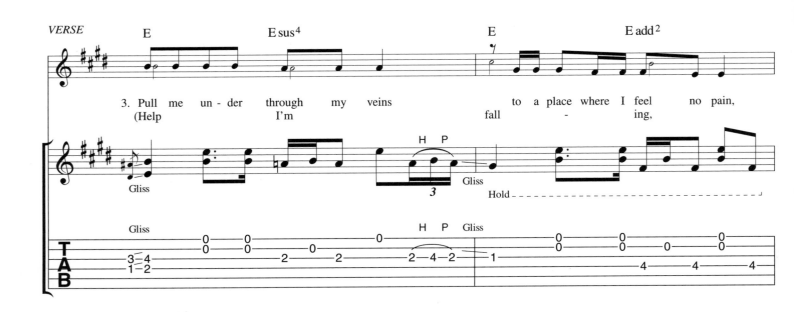

3. Pull me un - der through my veins to a place where I feel no pain,
(Help I'm fall - ing,

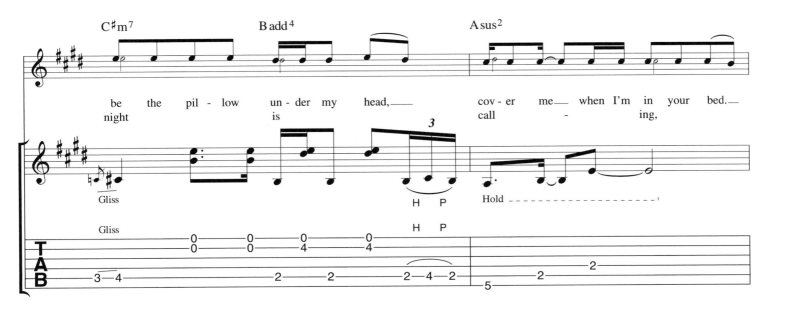

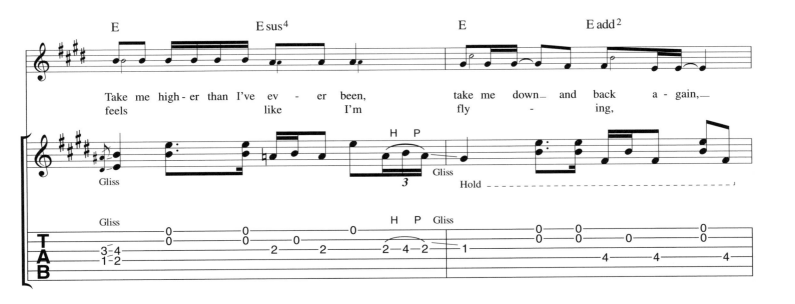

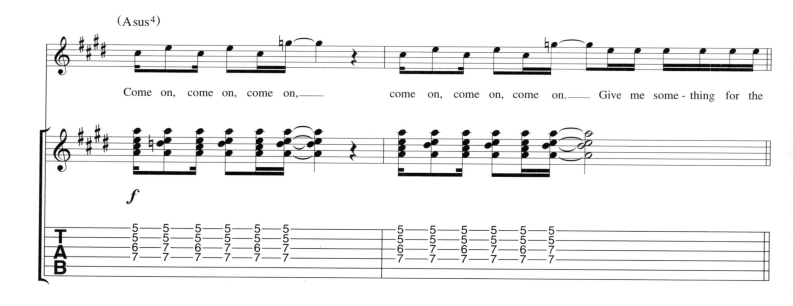

Come on, come on, come on,_____ come on, come on, come on._____ Give me some-thing for the

CHORUS

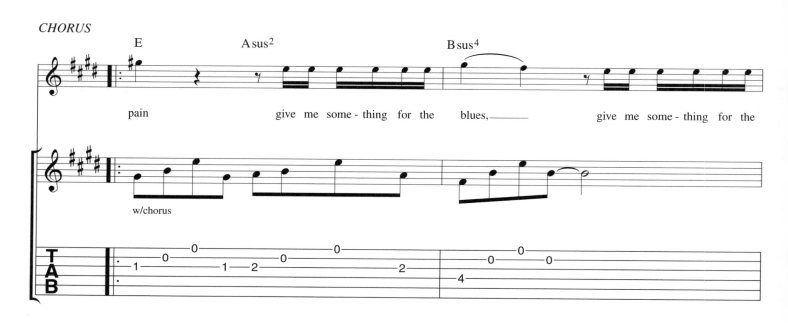

pain give me some-thing for the blues,_____ give me some-thing for the

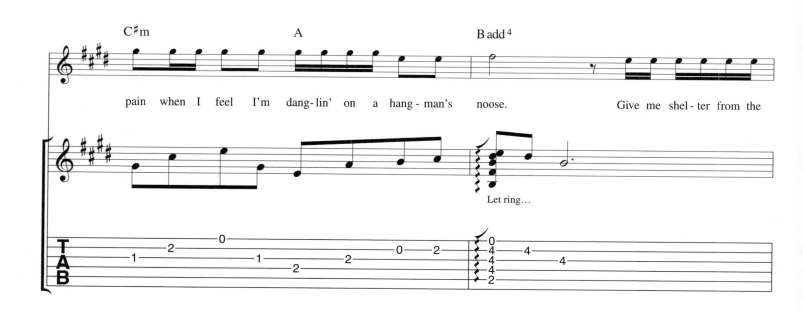

pain when I feel I'm dang-lin' on a hang-man's noose. Give me shel-ter from the

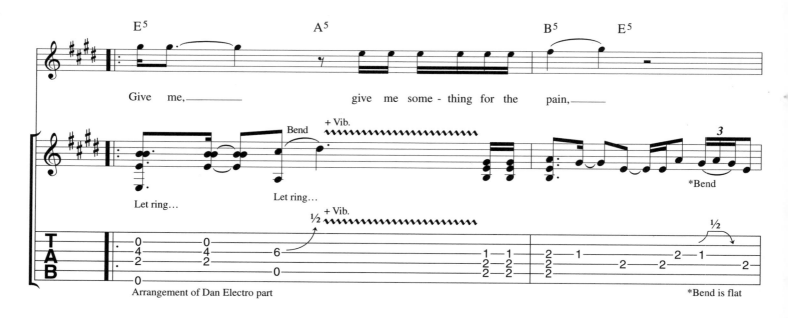

Give me,_____ give me some - thing for the pain,_____

Let ring... Let ring...

Arrangement of Dan Electro part   *Bend is flat

(1°) give me,_____ give me some - thing for the blues.

sim.

Verse 2:
Loneliness has found a home in me
My suitcase and guitar are my only family
I've tried to need someone like they needed me
Well, I opened up my heart but all I did was bleed
I don't need no lover just to get screwed
They don't make no bandage that's gonna cover my bruise.

This Ain't A Love Song

Words & Music by Jon Bon Jovi, Richie Sambora & Desmond Child

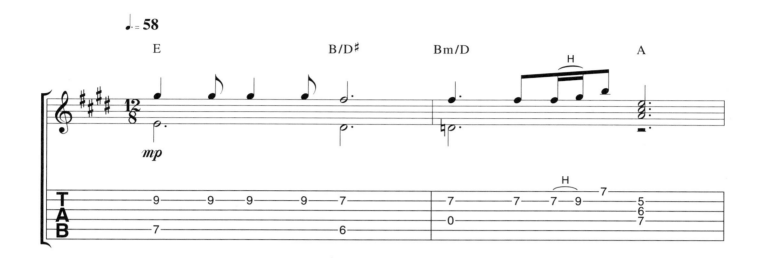

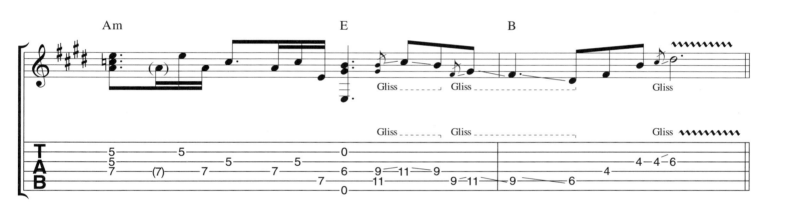

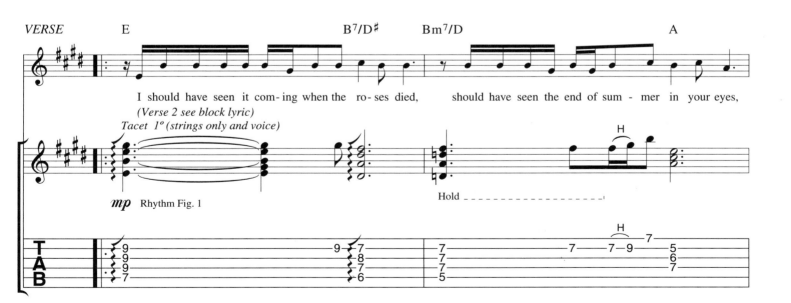

I should have seen it com-ing when the ro-ses died, should have seen the end of sum-mer in your eyes,

(Verse 2 see block lyric)

Tacet 1° (strings only and voice)

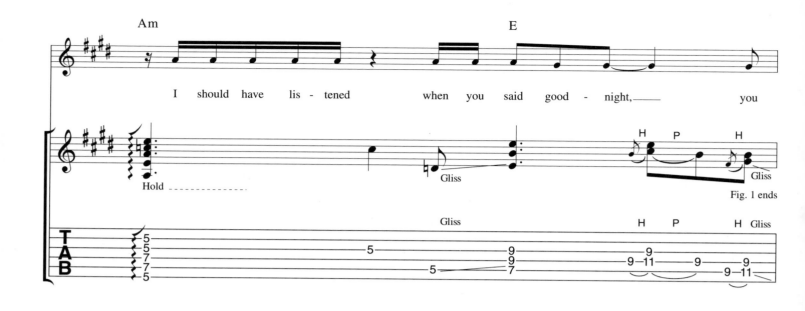

I should have lis - tened when you said good - night,_____ you

real - ly_____ meant good - bye._____

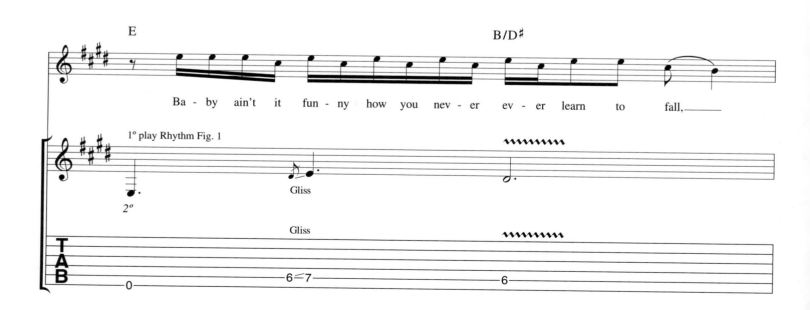

Ba - by ain't it fun - ny how you nev - er ev - er learn to fall,_____

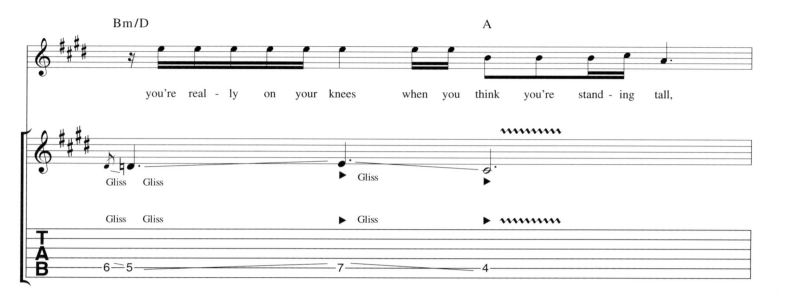

you're real - ly on your knees when you think you're stand - ing tall,

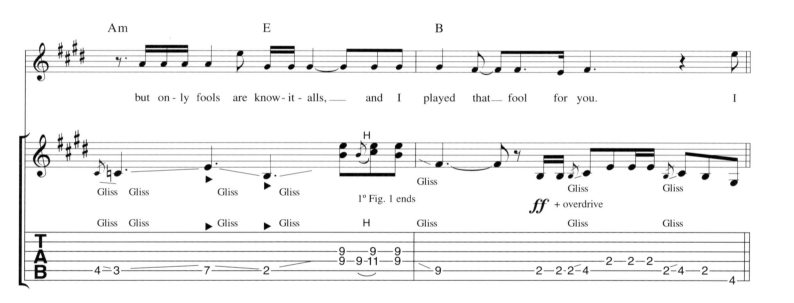

but on - ly fools are know - it - alls, ___ and I played that ___ fool for you. I

CHORUS

(1, 3.) cried and I cried, there were nights that I died for you ba - by, ___ I

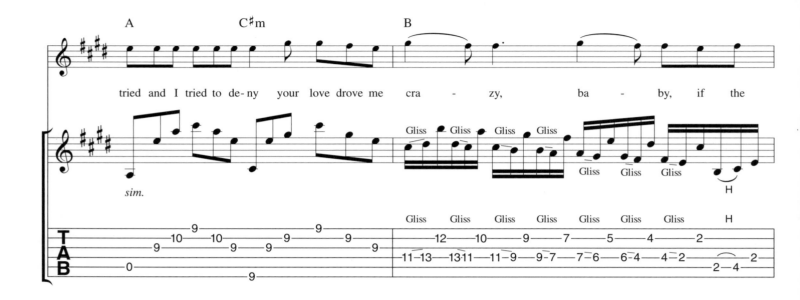

tried and I tried to de- ny your love drove me cra - zy, ba - by, if the

love that I got for you's gone,— and if the ri - ver I cried ain't that long,— then I'm

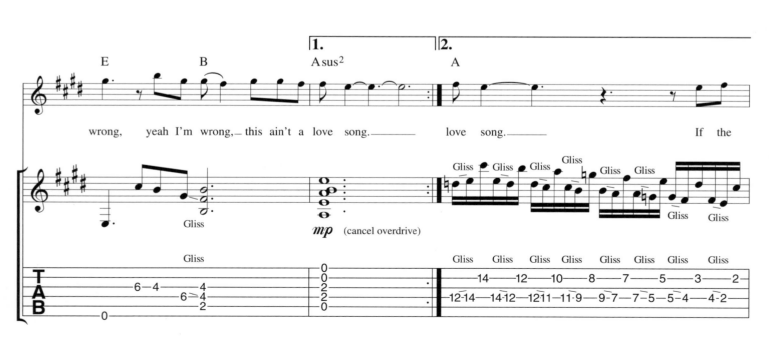

1.

2.

wrong, yeah I'm wrong,— this ain't a love song.———— love song.———— If the

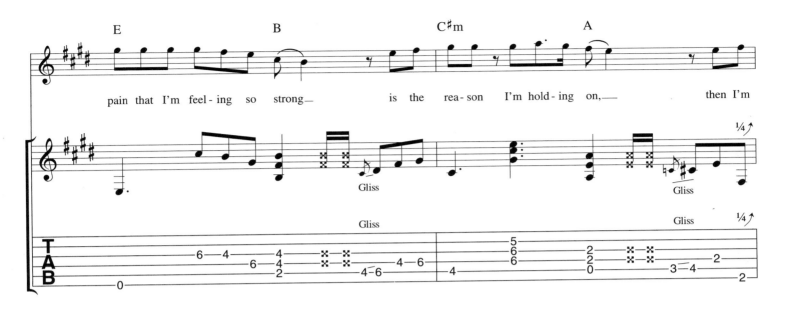

pain that I'm feel - ing so strong—— is the rea - son I'm hold - ing on,—— then I'm

To Coda ⊕

wrong, yeah I'm wrong,— this ain't a love song.——————

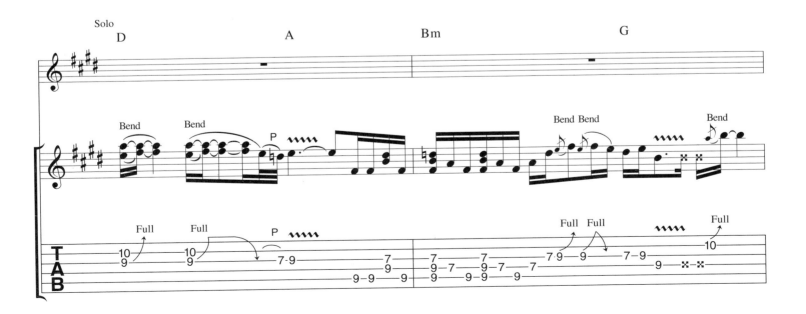

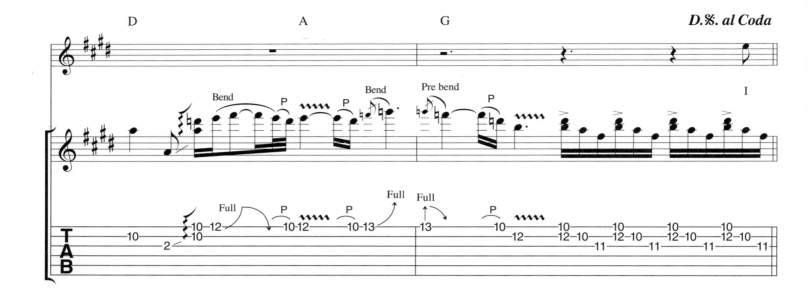

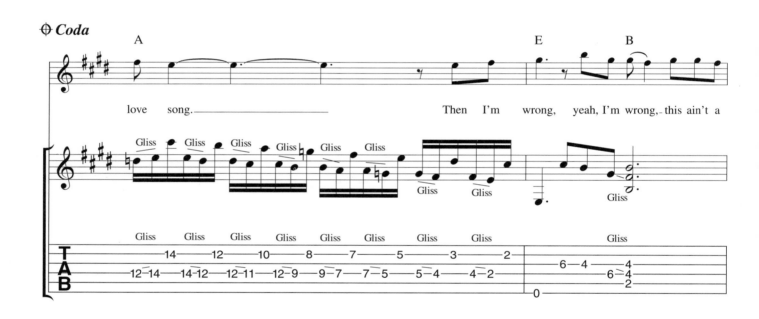

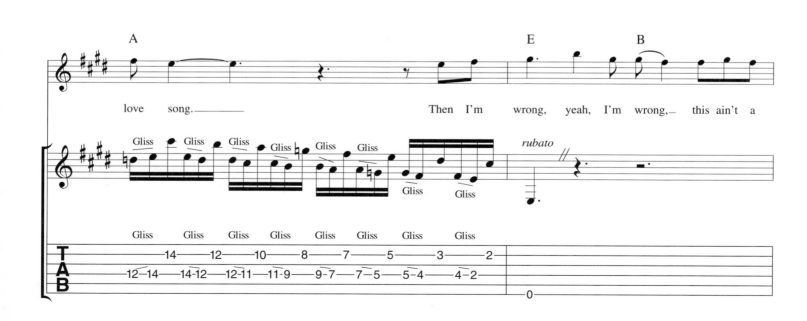

36

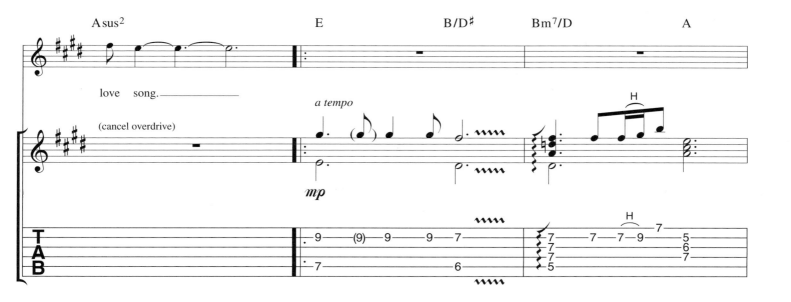

love   song._____

(cancel overdrive)

a tempo

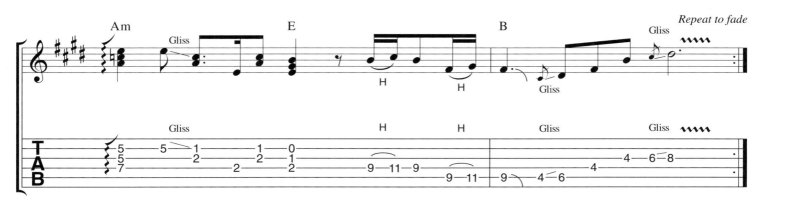

Repeat to fade

Verse 2:
Baby I thought you and me would stand the test of time
Like we got away with the perfect crime
But we were just a legend in my mind
I guess that I was blind.
Remember those nights dancing at the masquerade
The clowns wore smiles that wouldn't fade
You and I were renegades
Some things never change.

It made me so mad 'cause I wanted it bad for us baby
And now it's so sad that whatever we had ain't worth saving.

These Days

Words & Music by Jon Bon Jovi & Richie Sambora

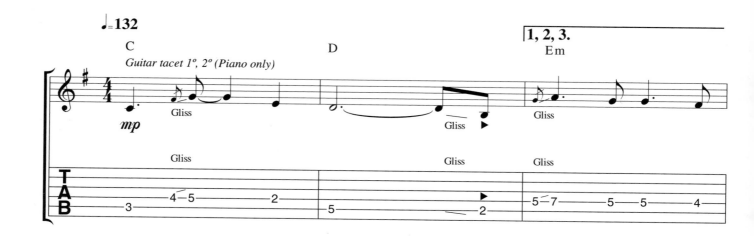

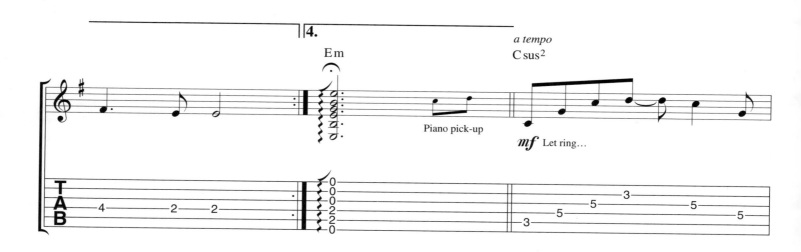

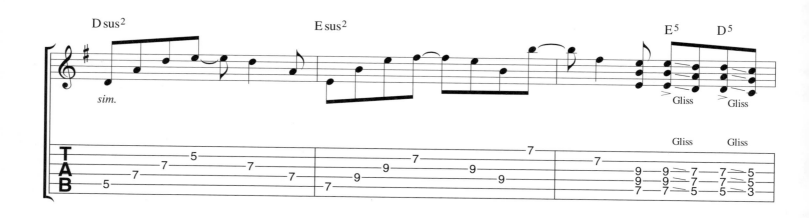

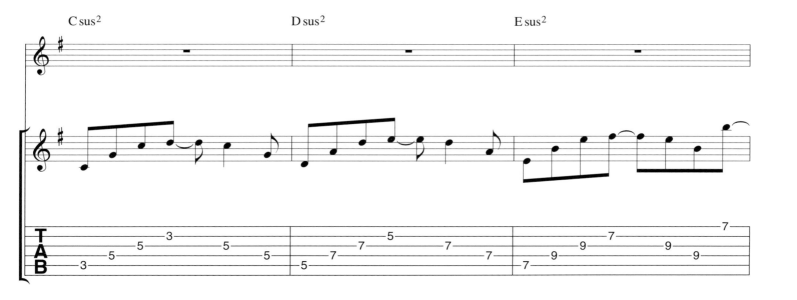

VERSE

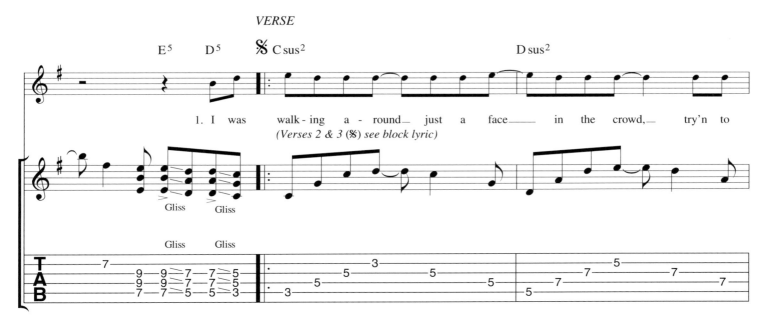

1. I was walk-ing a-round___ just a face___ in the crowd,___ try'n to
(Verses 2 & 3 (%) see block lyric)

Gliss   Gliss

Gliss   Gliss

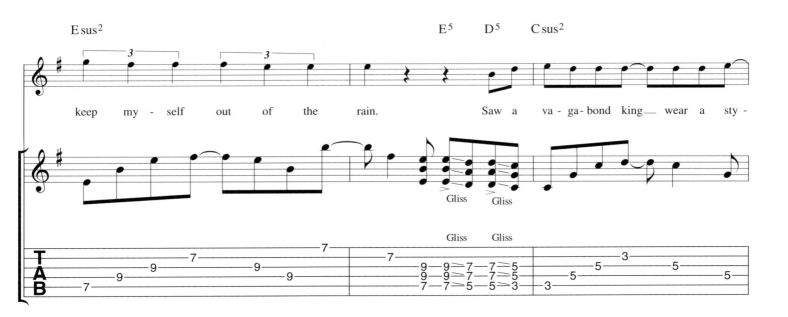

keep my-self out of the rain.   Saw a va-ga-bond king___ wear a sty-

Gliss   Gliss

Gliss   Gliss

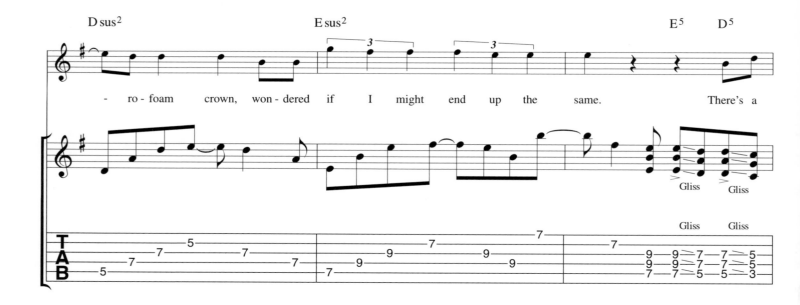

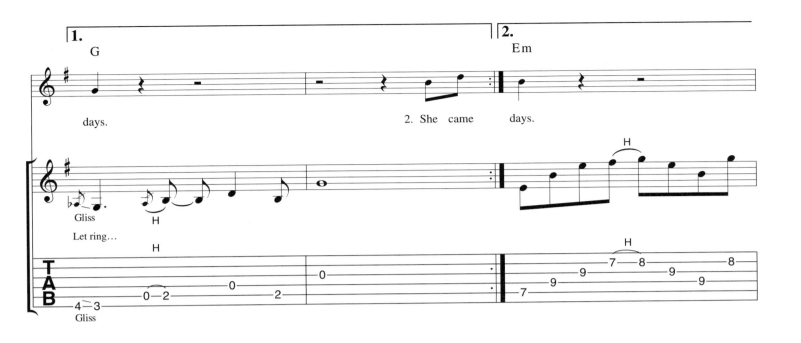

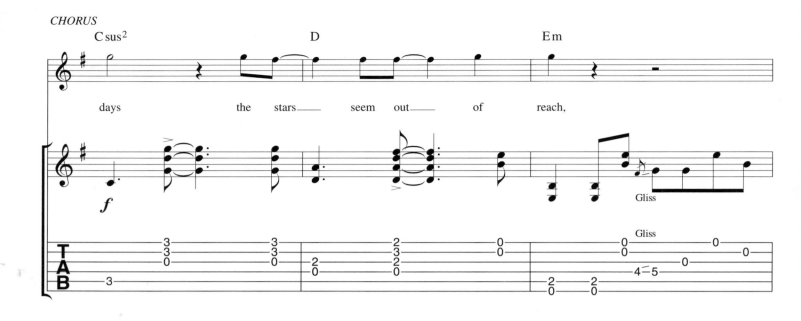

days   the   stars—— seem out—— of   reach,

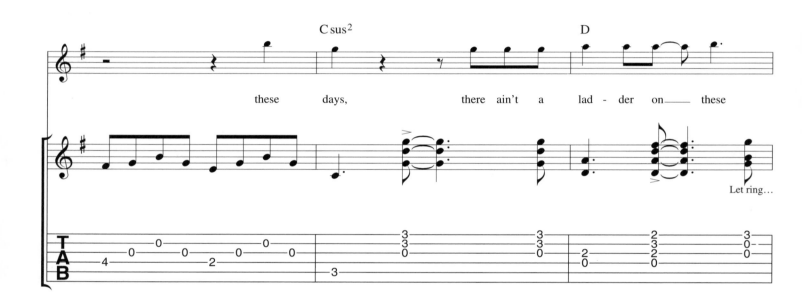

these   days,   there ain't a   lad - der on—— these

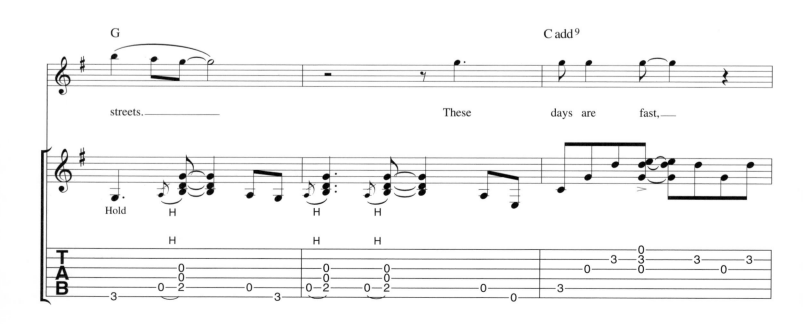

streets.——————   These   days are   fast,——

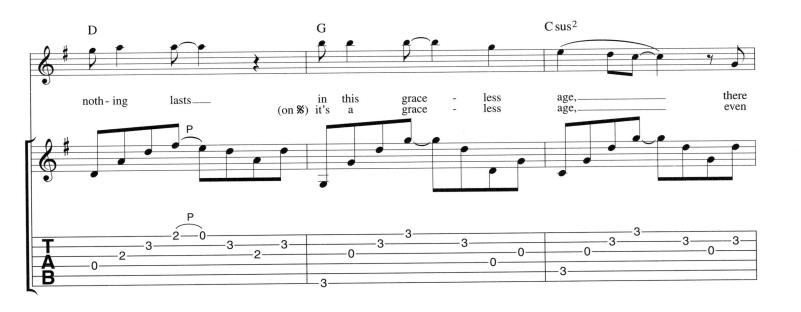

noth-ing lasts____ in this grace - less age,_____ there
(on 𝄋) it's a grace - less age,_____ even

To Coda ⊕   **D.𝄋. al Coda**

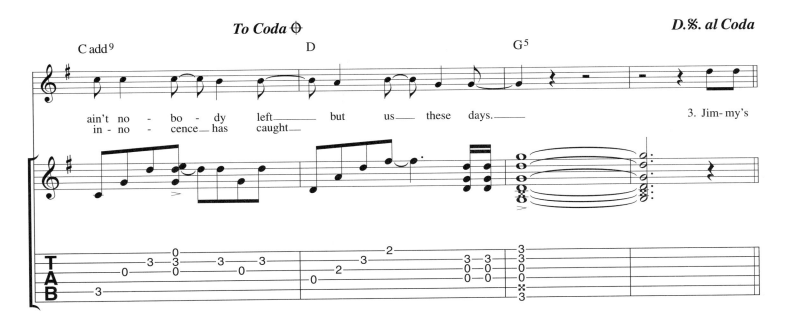

ain't no - bo - dy left____ but us____ these days.____
in - no - cence____ has caught____   3. Jim- my's

⊕ Coda

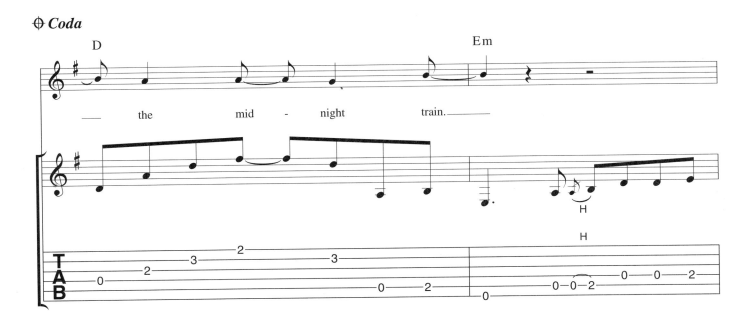

____ the mid - night train._____

There ain't no-bo-dy left___ but us___ these days.___

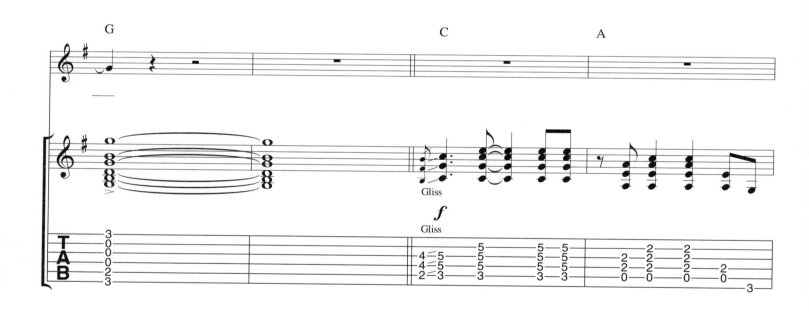

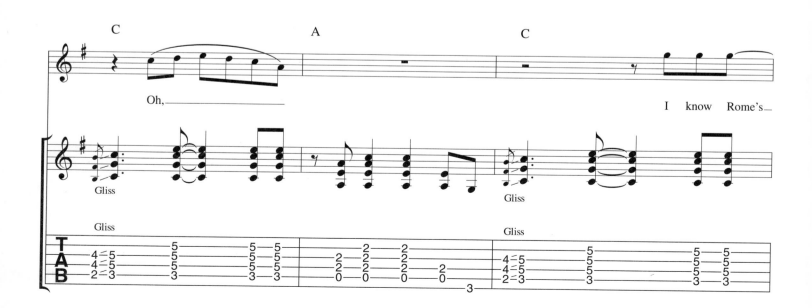

Oh,___

I know Rome's___

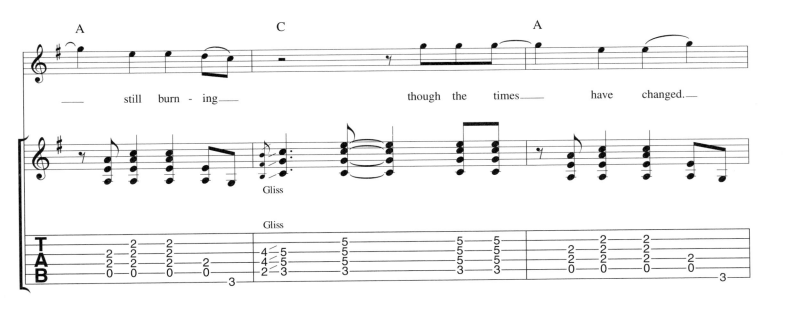

still burn - ing ___ though the times ___ have changed. ___

This world ___ keeps turn - ing round and round ___ and round ___

___ and round ___ these days.

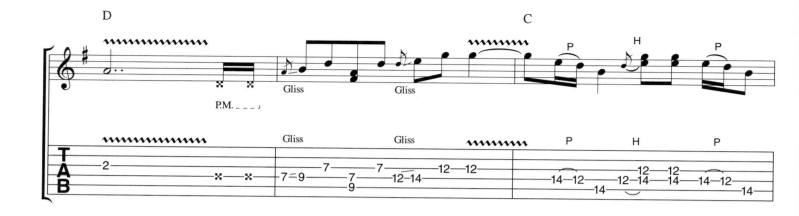

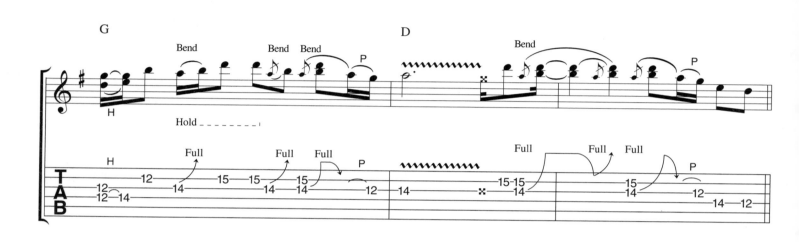

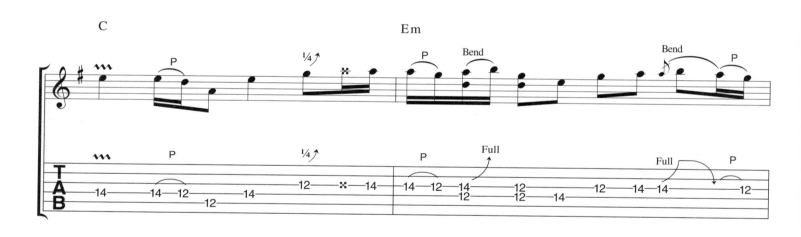

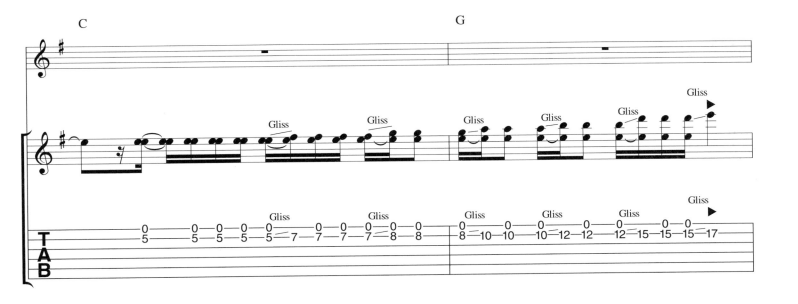

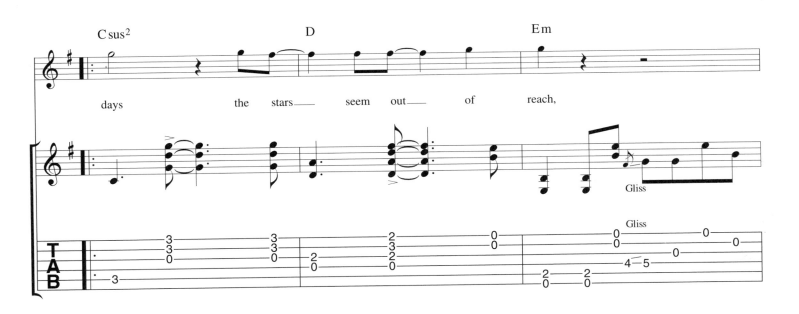

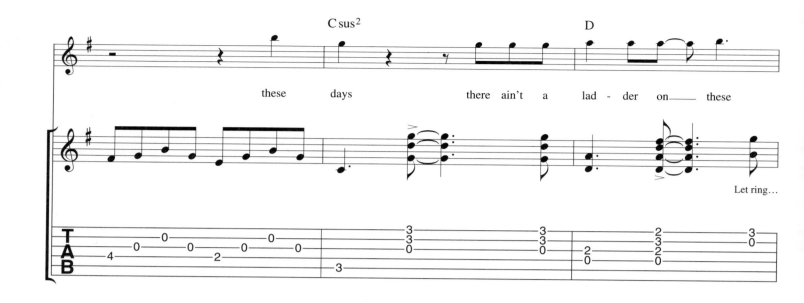

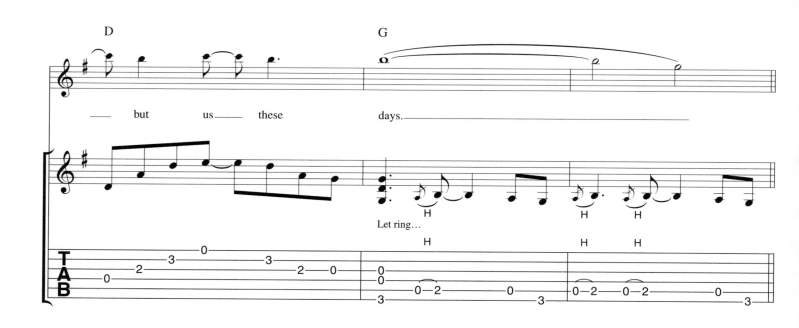

but   us____   these   days._____

Let ring…

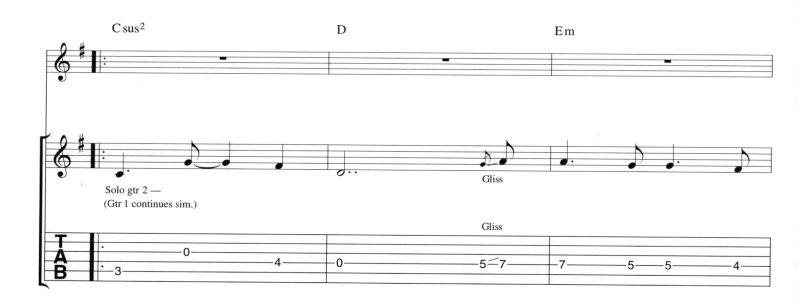

Solo gtr 2 —
(Gtr 1 continues sim.)

Gliss

Gliss

Ain't   no - bo - dy   left____   but   us____   these
(Vocal 1° only)

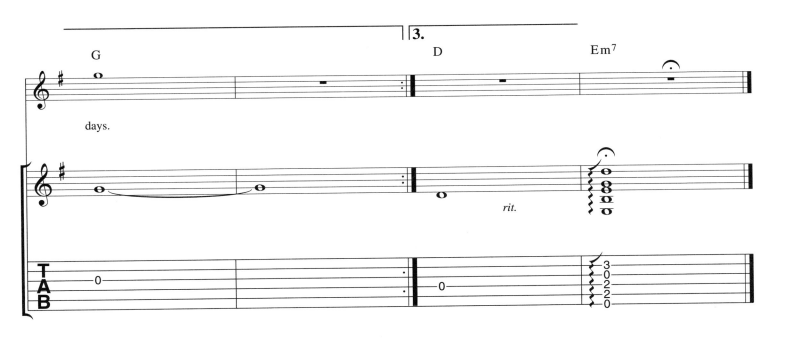

days.

rit.

Verse 2:
She came looking for some shelter
With a suitcase full of dreams
To a motel room on the boulevard
I guess she's trying to be James Dean
She's seen all the disciples and all the wanna-be's
No-one wants to be themselves these days.
Still there's nothing to hold onto but these days.

Verse 3: (%)
Jimmy's shoes busted both his legs
Trying to learn to fly
From a second storey window
He just jumped and closed his eyes
His mamma said he was crazy, he said "Momma I've got to try
Don't you know that all my heroes died
And I guess I'd rather die than fade away."

Lie To Me

Words & Music by Jon Bon Jovi & Richie Sambora

1. Ru-mour has it that your dad-dy's com-ing down, he's gon-na pay the rent,____
(Verses 2 & 3 see block lyric)

tell me ba-by is this as good as this life is gon-na get.____ It

feels like there's a stran - ger stand - ing in____ these shoes, but I

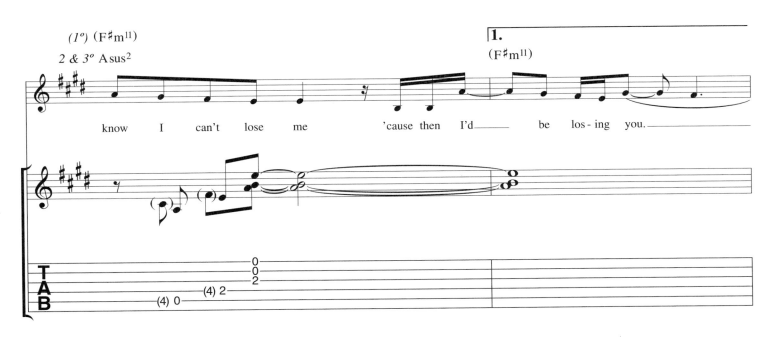

know I can't lose me 'cause then I'd____ be los - ing you.____

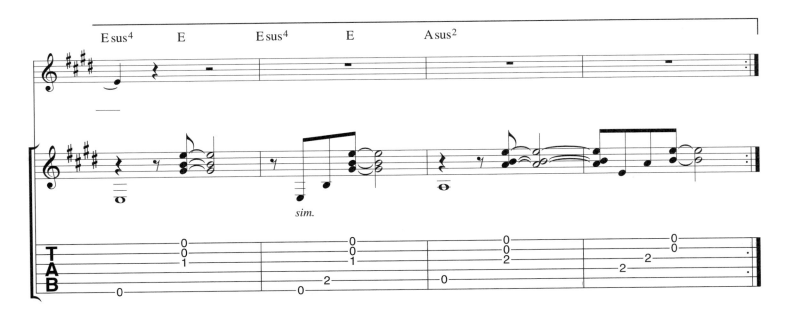

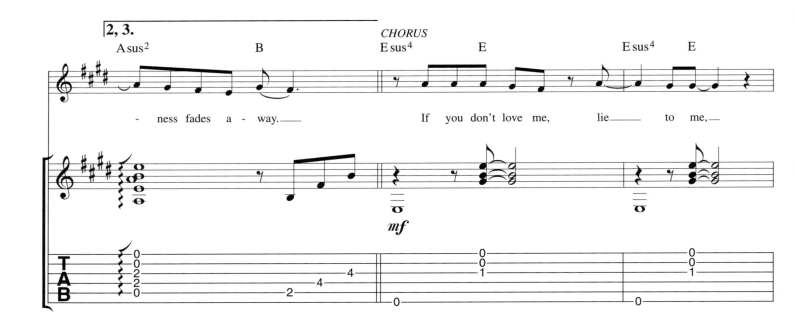

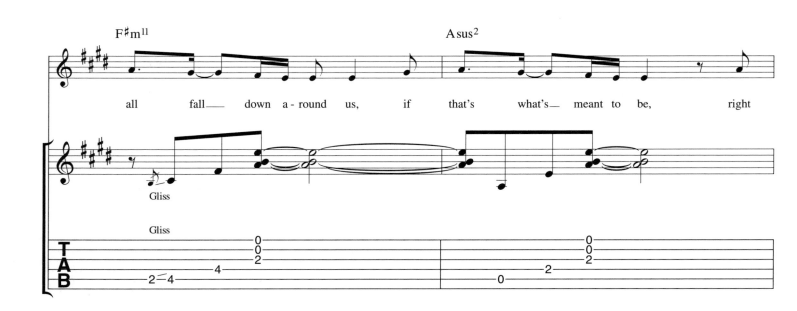

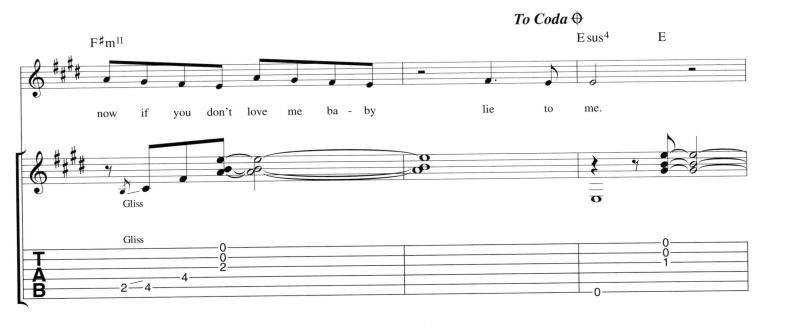

now if you don't love me ba - by   lie   to   me.

me.

Oh.———

Synth. arr. for gtr

Hold chord…

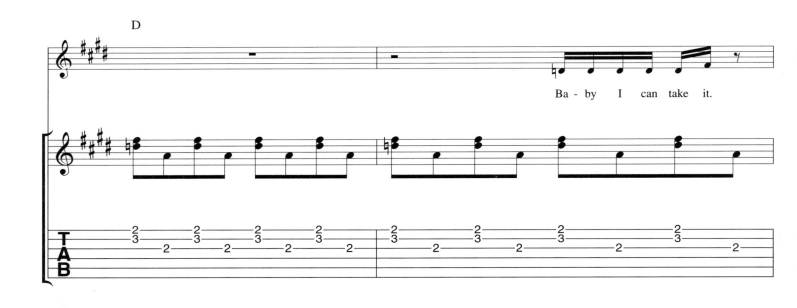

Ba - by I can take it.

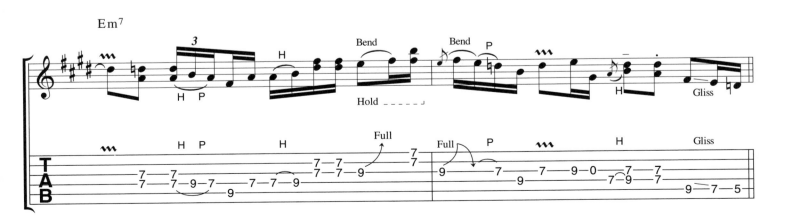

It's a bitch but life's a rol - ler coast - er ride,

the ups and downs will make you scream some - time, it's hard be - liev - ing that the

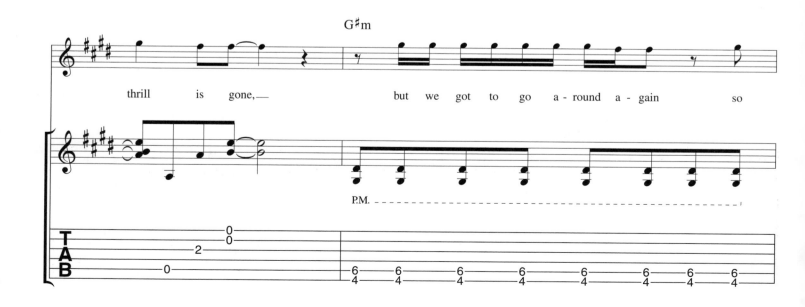

thrill is gone, but we got to go a - round a - gain so

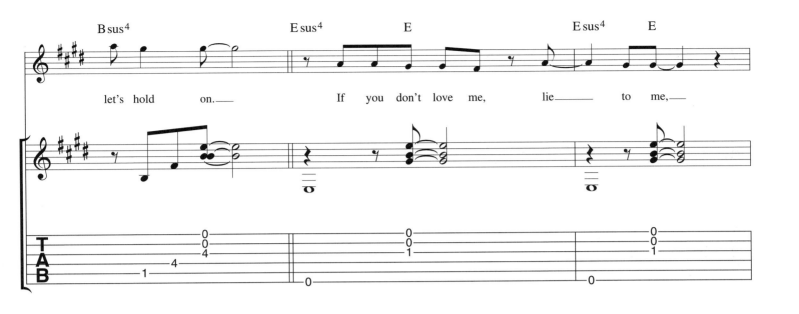

let's hold on.___ If you don't love me, lie___ to me,___

'cause ba-by you're the one thing I___ be-lieve,___ let it all fall___ down a-round us, if

that's what's_ meant to be, right now if you don't love me ba-by lie to

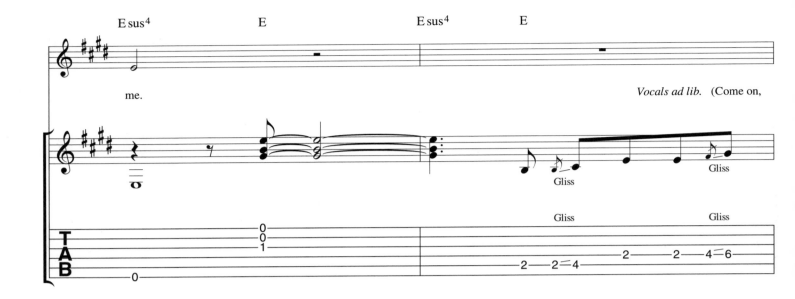

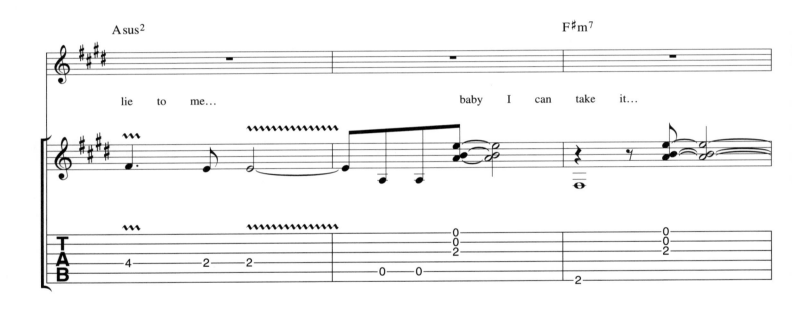

Verse 2:
I know I promised baby I would be the one
To make our dreams come true.
I ain't too proud of all the struggles and the hard times
We've been through
When this cold world comes between us
Please tell me you'll be brave
'Cause I can realise the danger
When forgiveness fades away.

Verse 3(%):
Pour another cup of coffee babe
I got something to say to you
Well I ain't got the winning ticket
Not the one that's gonna pull us through
No one said that it'd be easy
Let your old man take you home
But know if you walk out on me
That darling I'd be gone.

Damned

Words & Music by Jon Bon Jovi & Richie Sambora

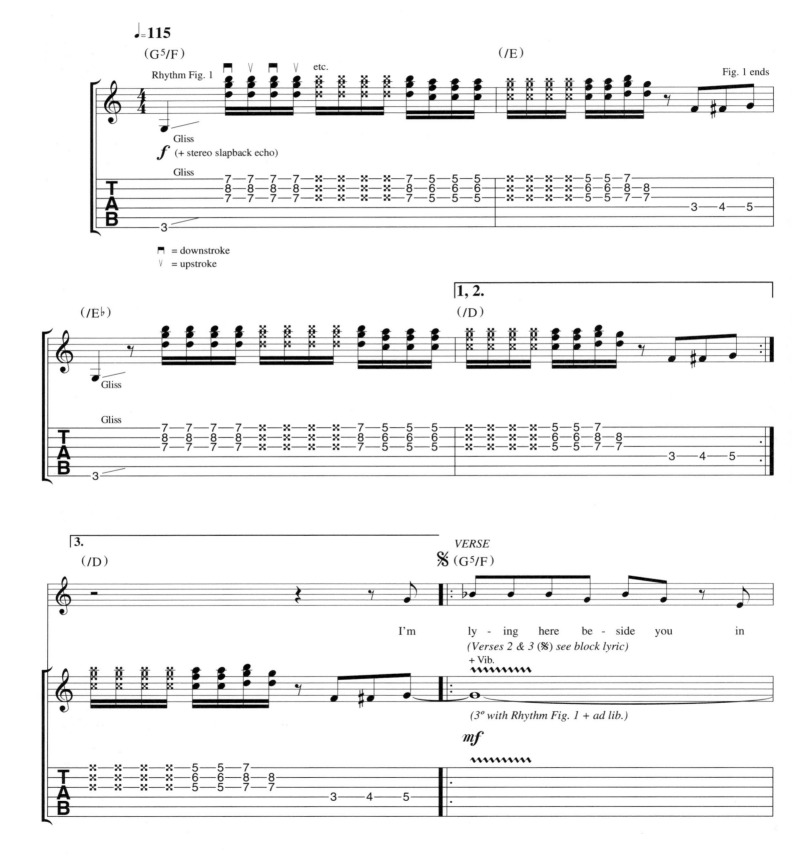

= downstroke

= upstroke

I'm ly-ing here be-side you in

(Verses 2 & 3 (𝄊) see block lyric)

(3° with Rhythm Fig. 1 + ad lib.)

(/E)   (/Eb)   (/D)

some-one el - se's bed,___ know - ing what we're do - ing's wrong but bet - ter left un - said. Your

Bend

Full

(/F)   (/E)   (/Eb)

breath - ing sounds like scream - ing, it's all that I can stand,___ his ring is on your fin - ger but my

P

Bend

Full

P

CHORUS

(/D)   G⁵

heart is in your hands. Damned if you love___ me,

etc.

f

(2° Play Rhythm Fig 1)

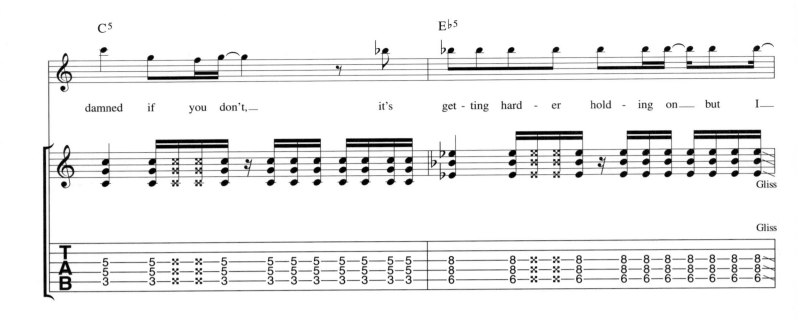

damned if you don't,— it's get-ting hard - er hold-ing on— but I—

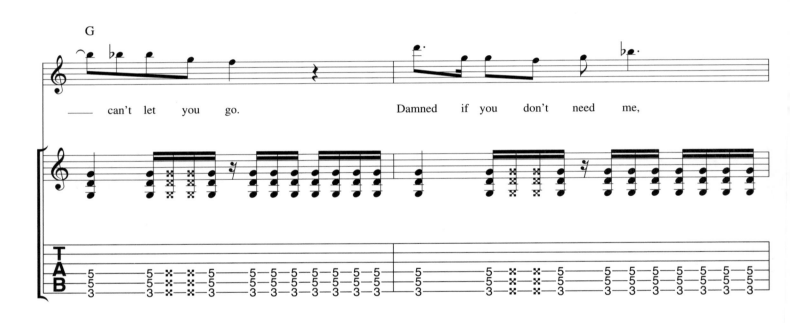

— can't let you go. Damned if you don't need me,

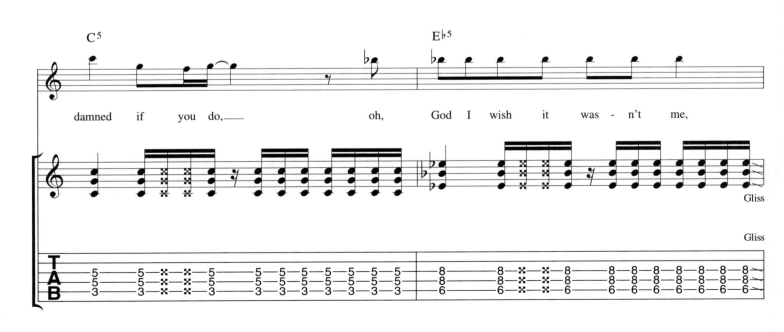

damned if you do,— oh, God I wish it was - n't me,

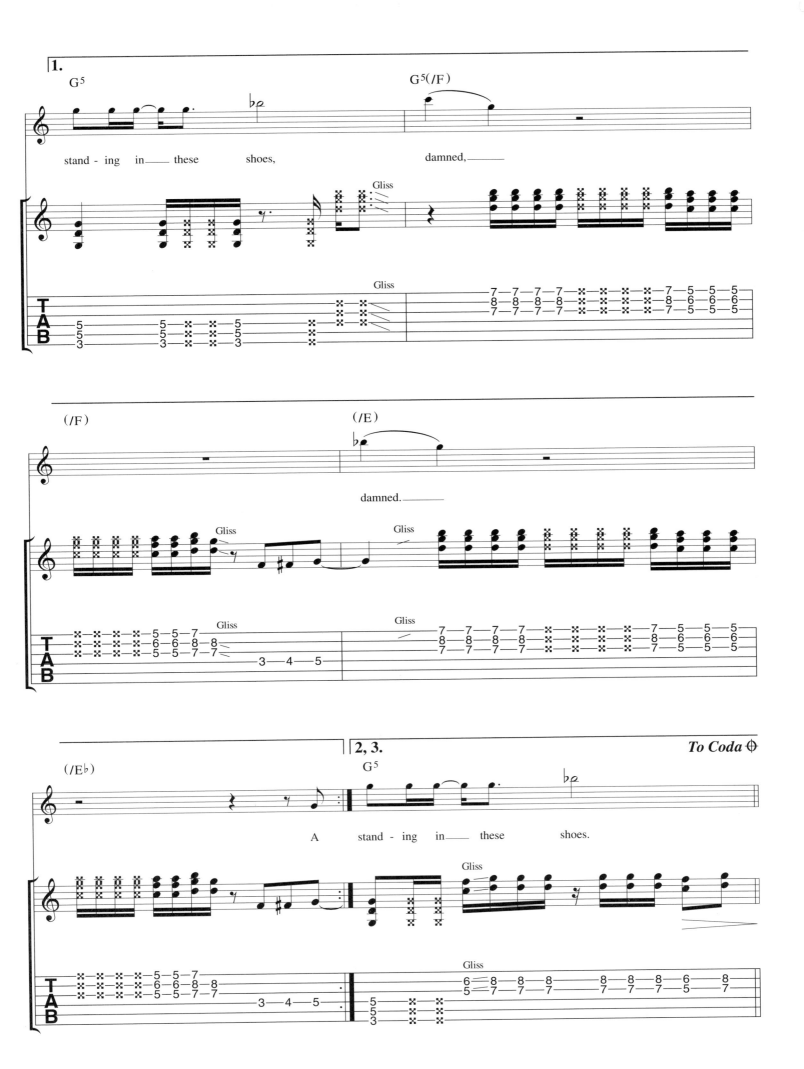

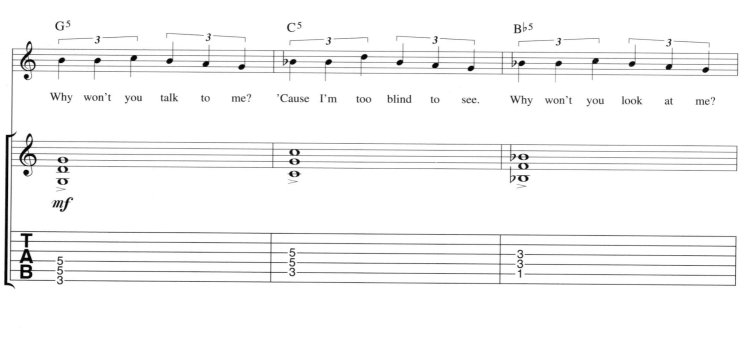

Why won't you talk to me? 'Cause I'm too blind to see. Why won't you look at me?

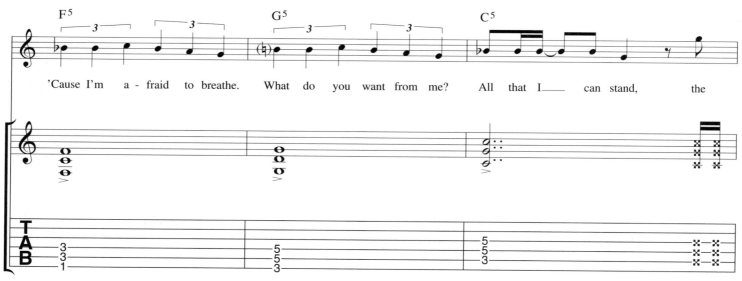

'Cause I'm a-fraid to breathe. What do you want from me? All that I___ can stand, the

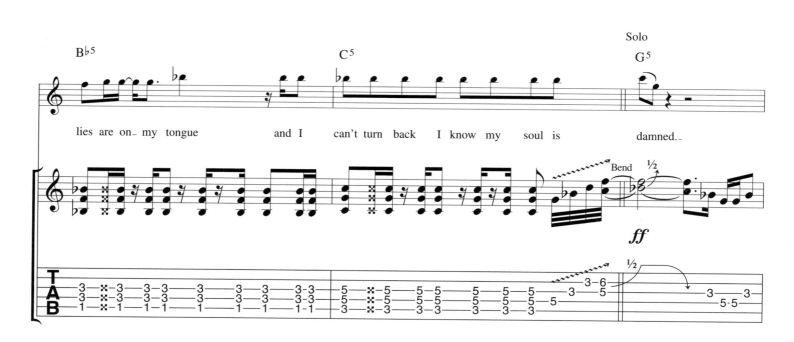

lies are on_ my tongue and I can't turn back I know my soul is damned._

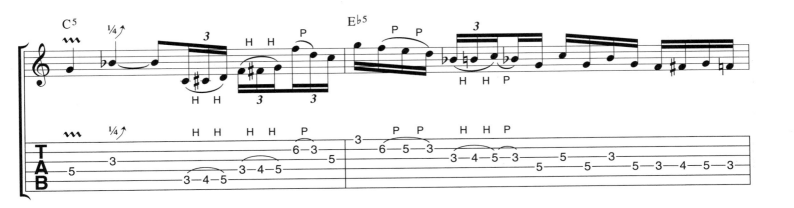

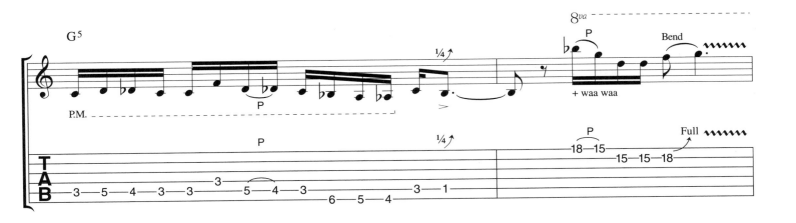

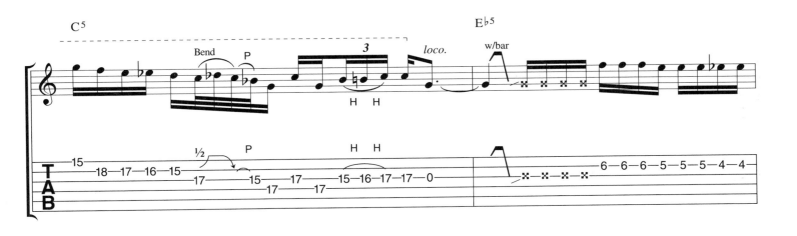

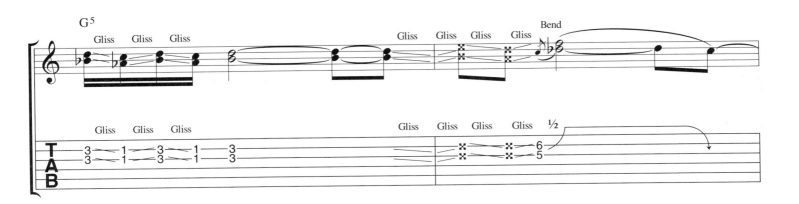

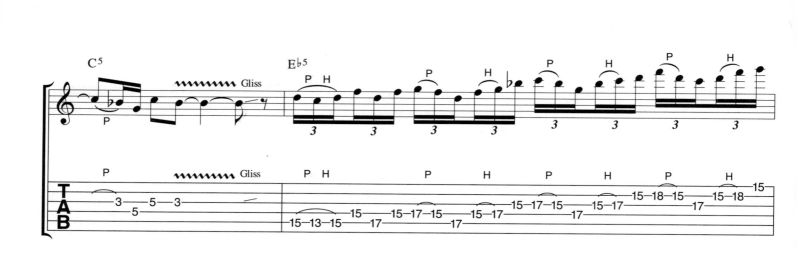

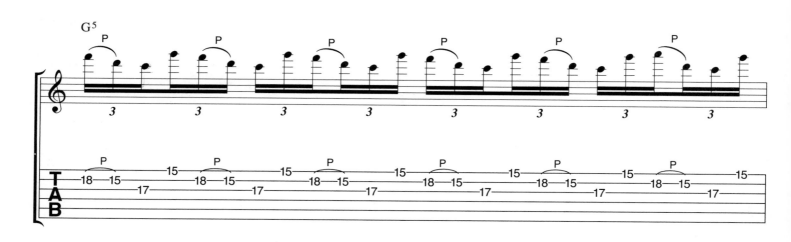

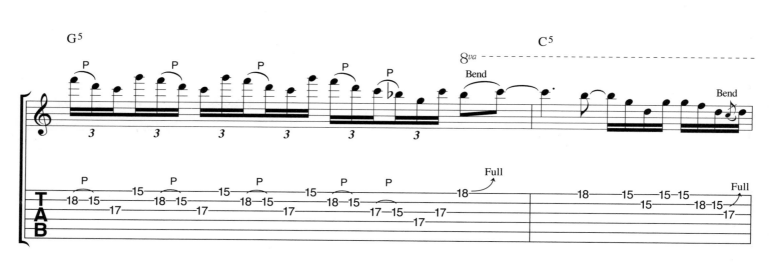

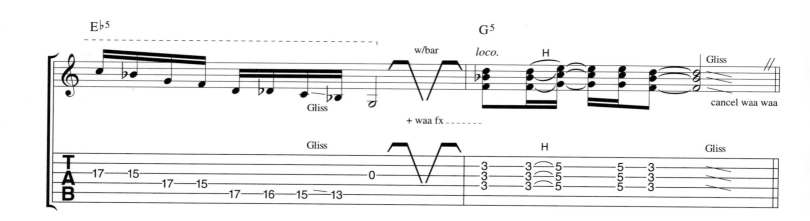

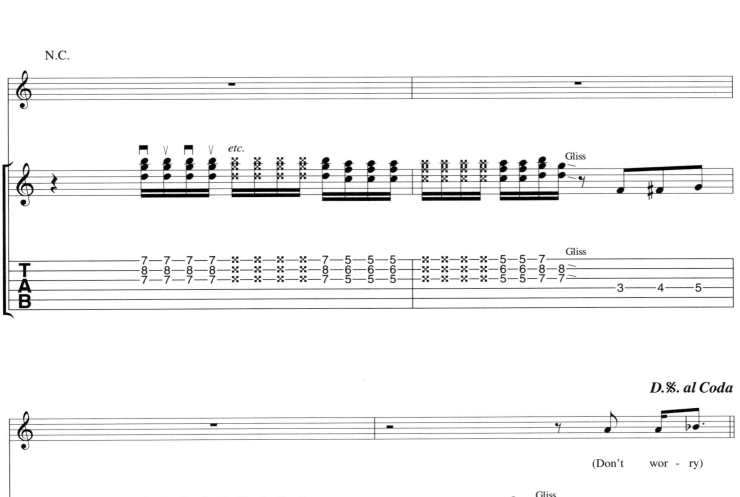

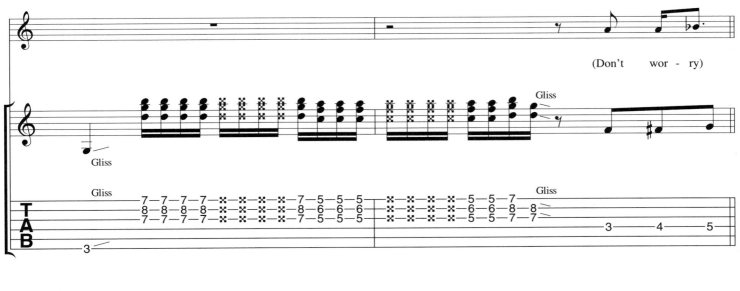

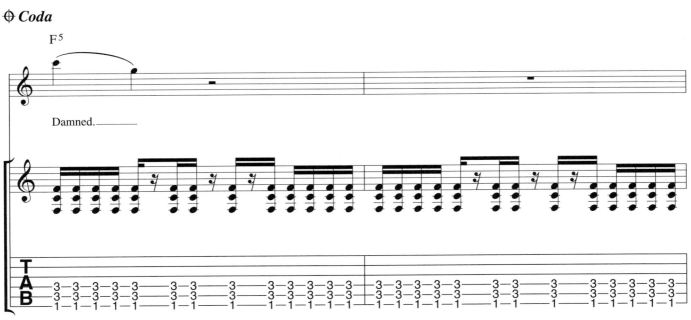

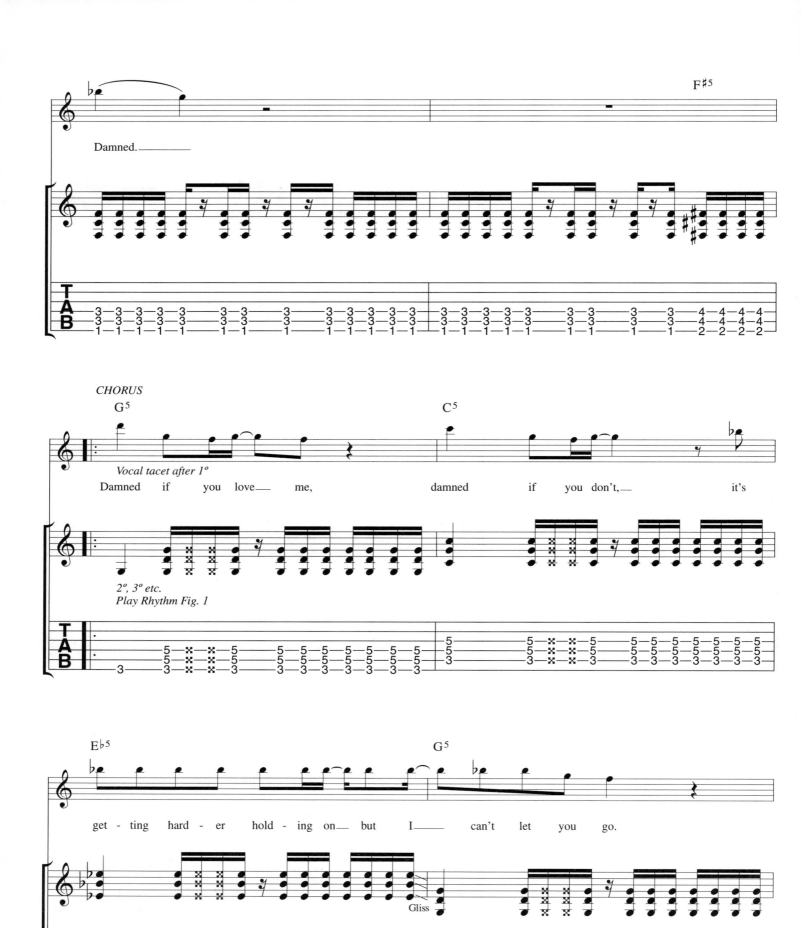

F#5

Damned.____

CHORUS
G5   C5

Vocal tacet after 1°
Damned   if   you   love____   me,   damned   if   you   don't,____   it's

2°, 3° etc.
Play Rhythm Fig. 1

Eb5   G5

get - ting   hard - er   hold - ing   on____   but   I____   can't   let   you   go.

Gliss

Gliss

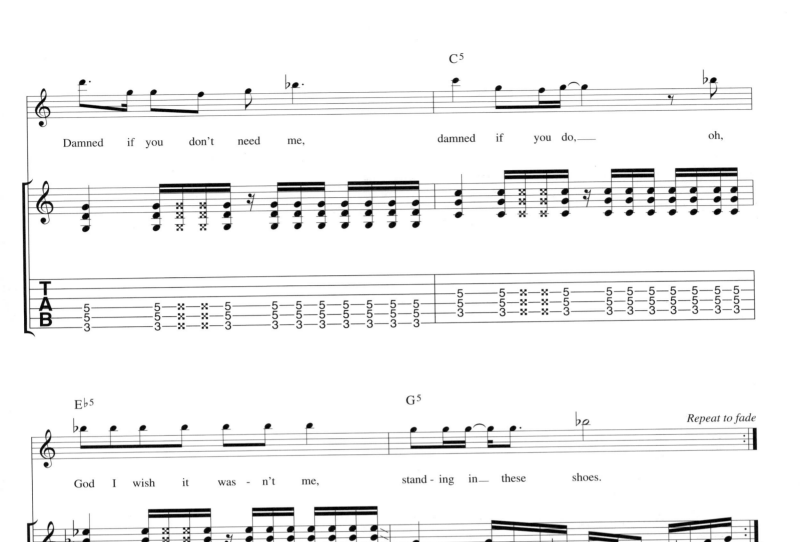

Damned if you don't need me, damned if you do,— oh,

God I wish it was-n't me, stand-ing in— these shoes.

Repeat to fade

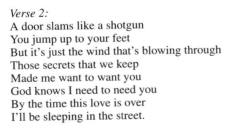

Verse 2:
A door slams like a shotgun
You jump up to your feet
But it's just the wind that's blowing through
Those secrets that we keep
Made me want to want you
God knows I need to need you
By the time this love is over
I'll be sleeping in the street.

Verse 3 (%):
I ain't gonna call you
Or hear you say my name
And if you see me on the streets
Don't wave, just walk away
Our lives are getting twisted
Let's keep our stories straight
The more that I resist it
My temptation turns to fate.

My Guitar Lies Bleeding In My Arms

Words & Music by Jon Bon Jovi & Richie Sambora

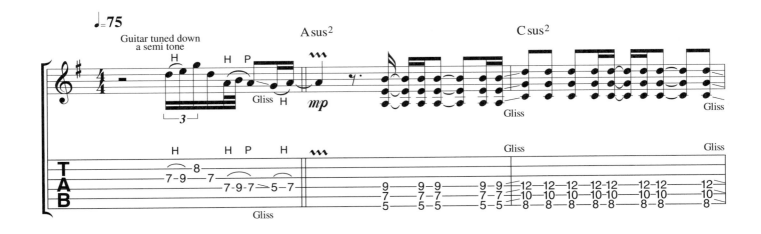

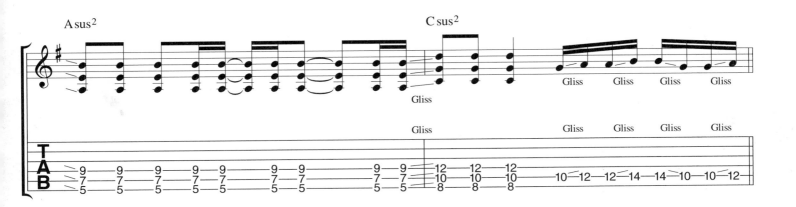

1. Mi - se - ry— likes com - pa - ny,— I like the way— that sounds,— I've been
(Verses 2 & 3 (%) see block lyric)

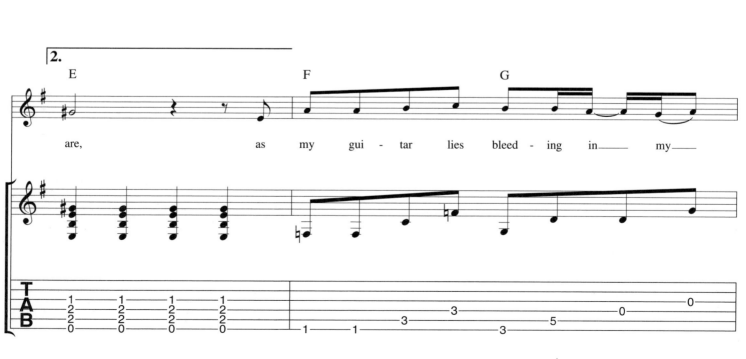

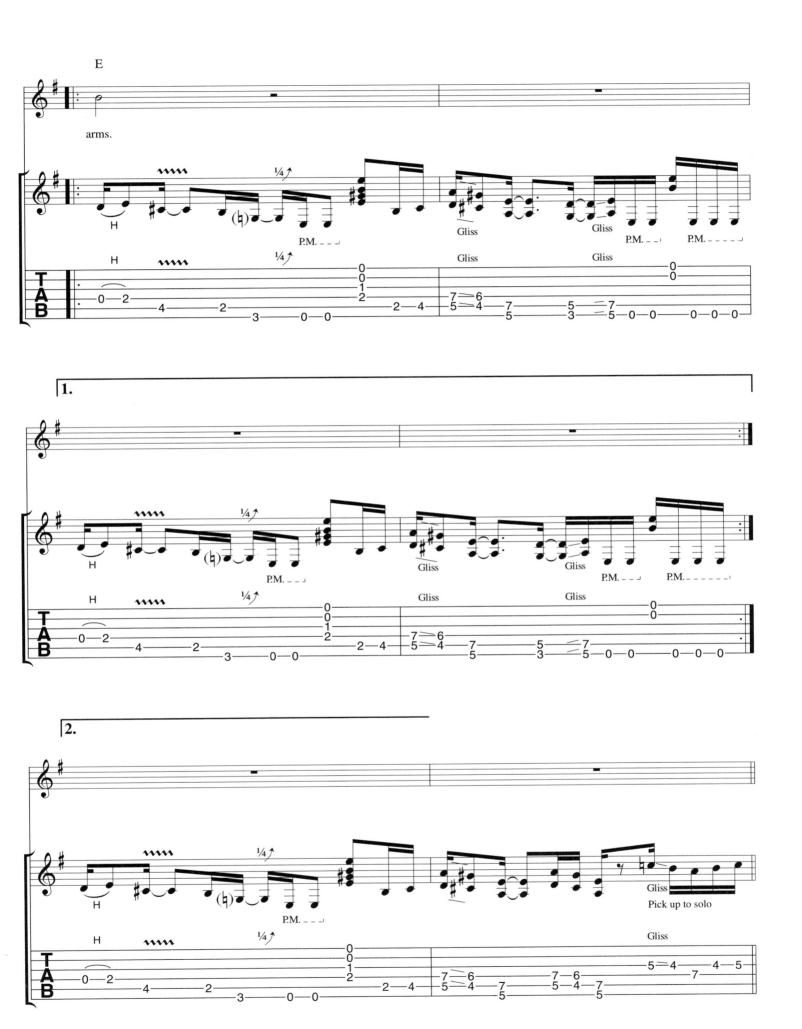

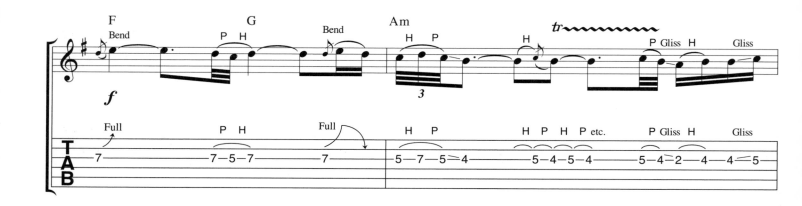

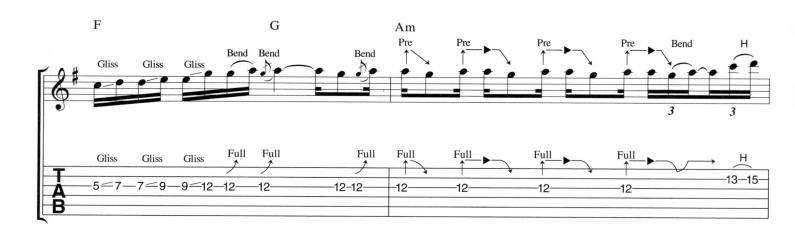

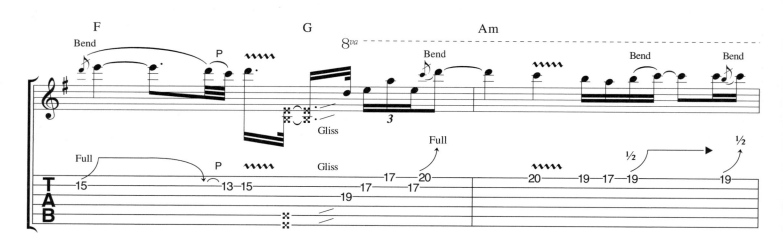

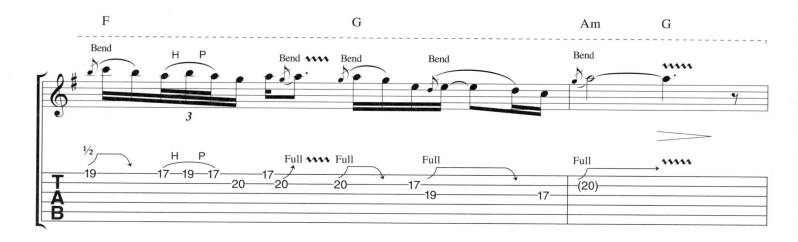

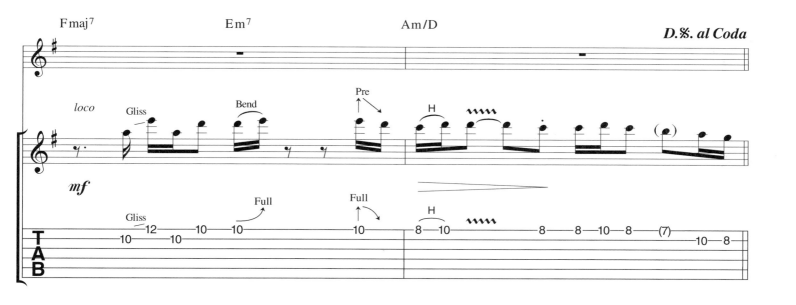

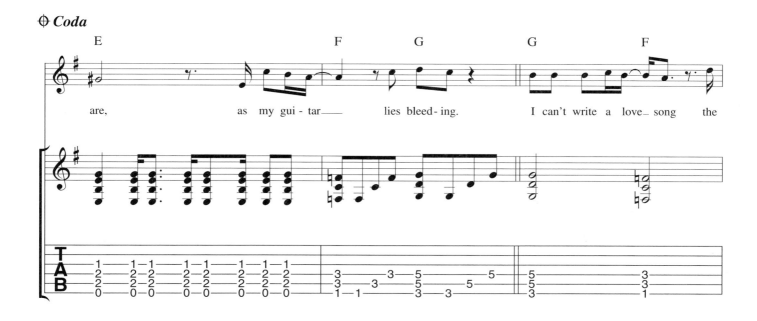

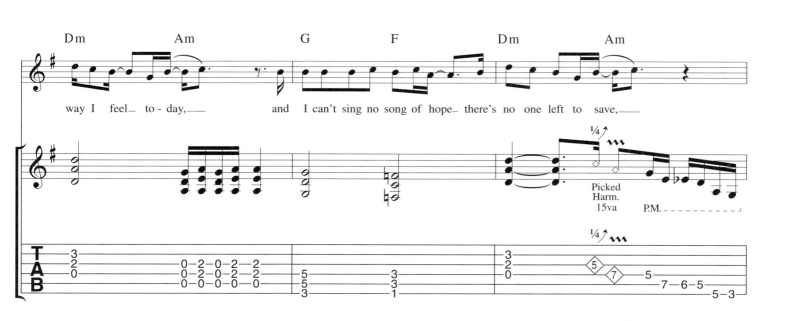

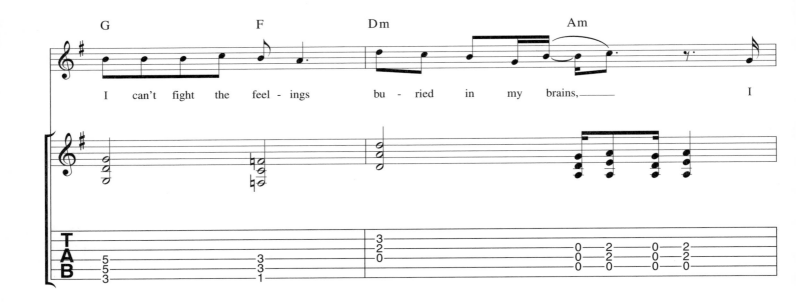

I can't fight the feel - ings bu - ried in my brains,_____ I

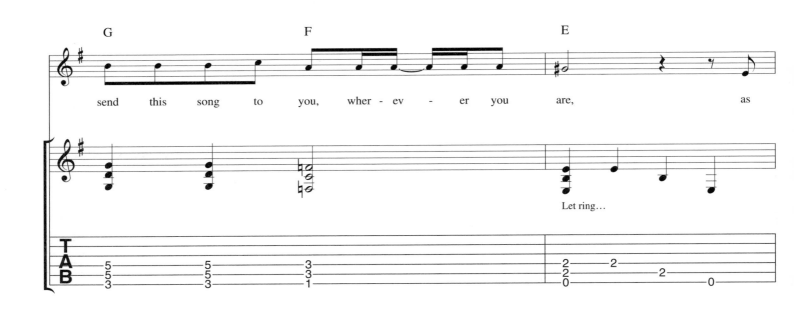

send this song to you, wher - ev - er you are, as

Let ring…

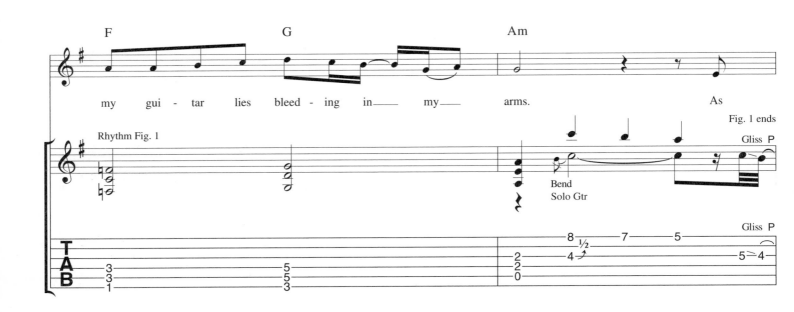

my gui - tar lies bleed - ing in_____ my_____ arms. As

Fig. 1 ends

Rhythm Fig. 1

Gliss P

Bend
Solo Gtr

Gliss P

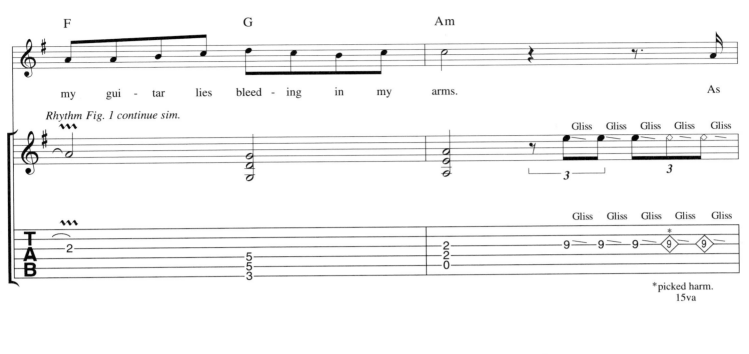

my gui - tar lies bleed - ing in my arms.   As

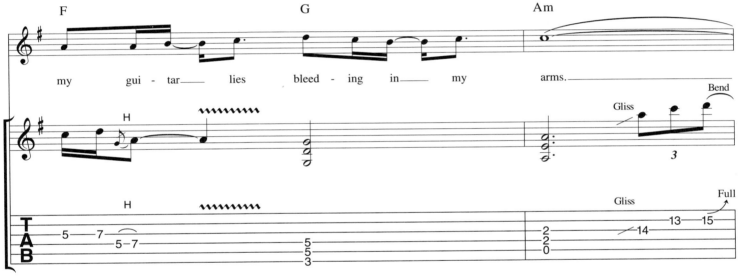

my gui - tar___ lies bleed - ing in___ my arms.___

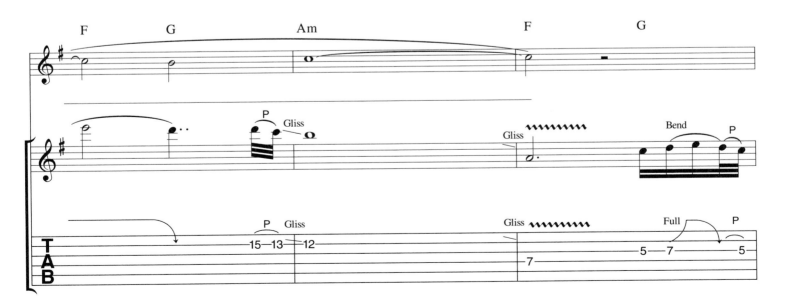

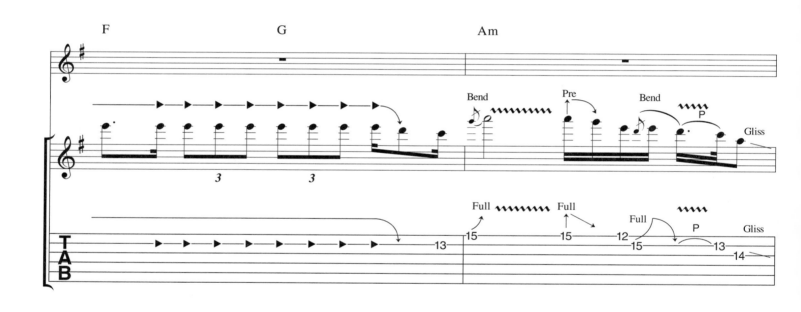

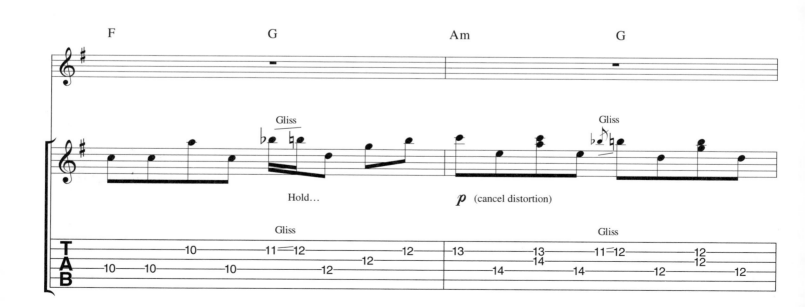

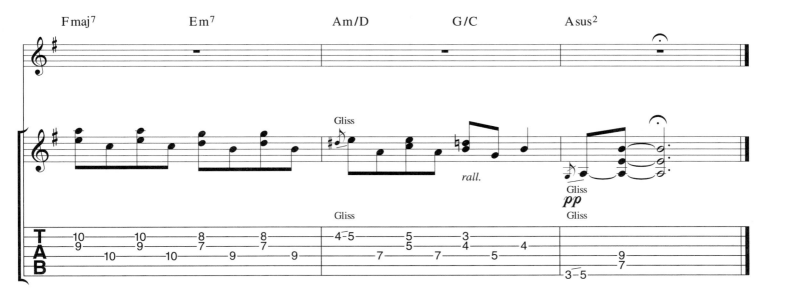

Verse 2:
I'm tired of watching T.V., it makes me want to scream
Outside the world is burning, man it's hard to believe
Each day you know you're dying from the cradle to the grave
I get so numb sometimes that I can't feel the pain.

I can't write a love song the way I feel today
I can't sing no song of hope I got nothing to say
Life is feeling kind of strange, it's strange enough these days
I sing this song to you whoever you are
As my guitar lies bleeding in my arms.

Verse 3 (𝄋):
Staring at the paper, I don't know what to write
I'll have my last cigarette, we'll turn out the lights
Maybe tomorrow I'll feel a different way
But here in my confusion I don't know what to say.

I can't write a love song the way I feel today
I can't sing no song of hope I got nothing to say
I can't fight the feelings that are burning in my veins
I send this song to you wherever you are
As my guitar lies bleeding. . .

(It's Hard) Letting You Go

Words & Music by Jon Bon Jovi

*Throughout, hold chords and let notes ring

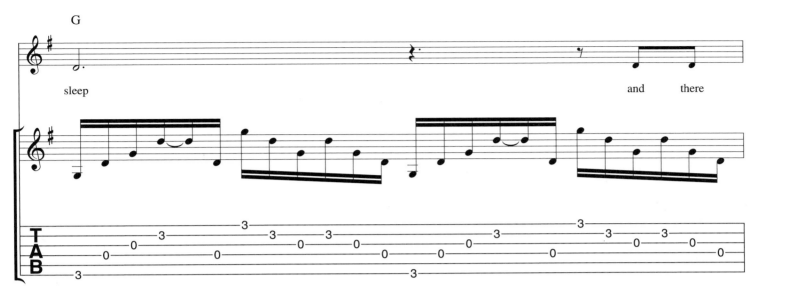

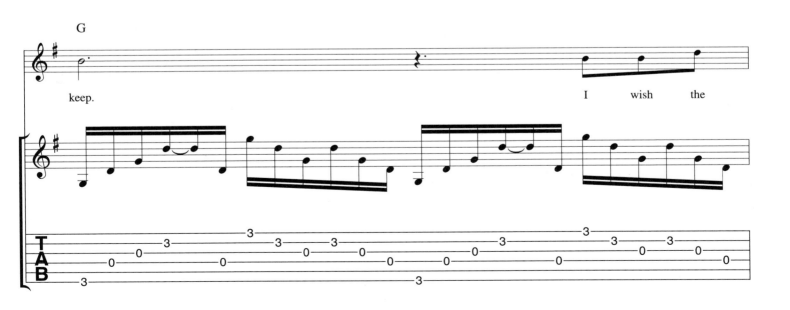

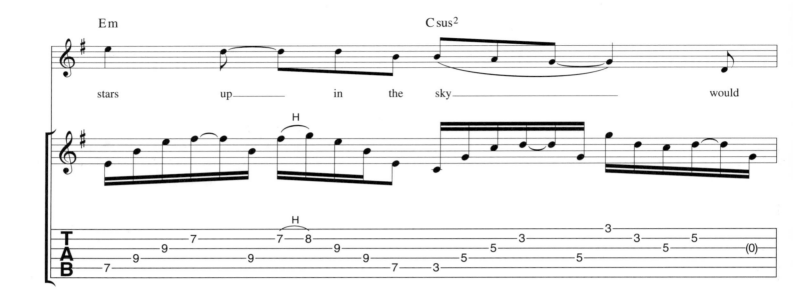

stars   up———   in the   sky————————————————   would

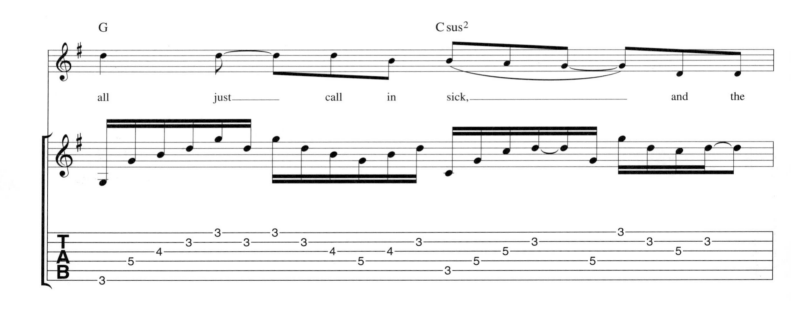

all   just————   call   in   sick,——————————————   and   the

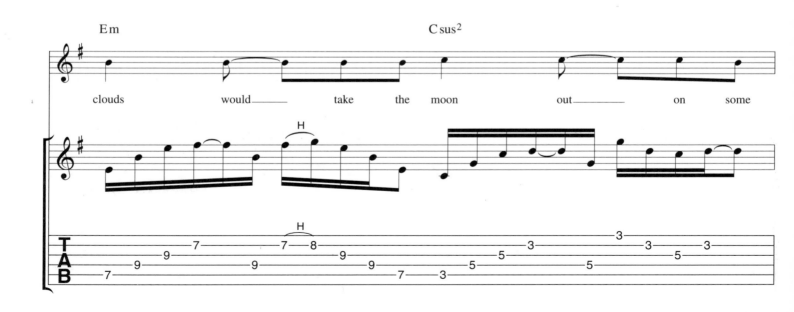

clouds   would————   take   the   moon   out————————   on   some

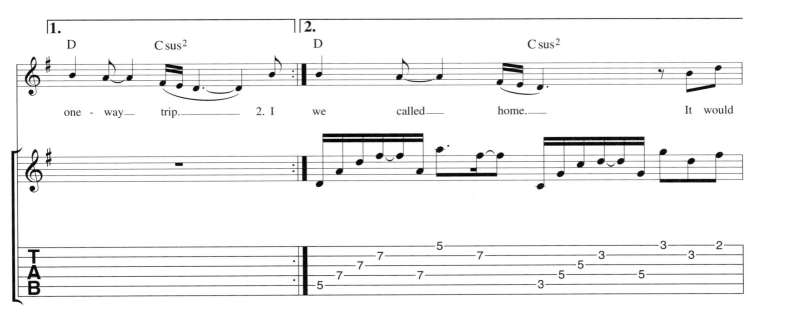

one - way trip. 2. I we called home. It would

all have been so ea - sy, if you'd on - ly made me cry and

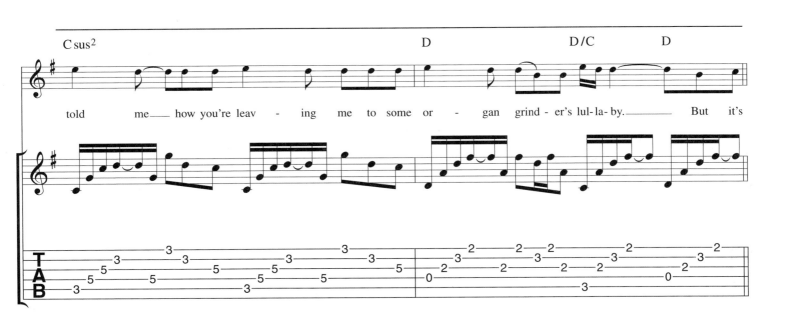

told me how you're leav - ing me to some or - gan grind - er's lul - la - by. But it's

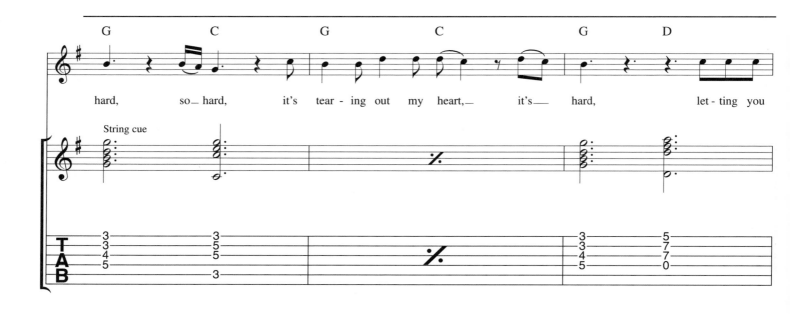

hard,   so— hard,   it's   tear - ing out   my   heart,—   it's— hard,   let - ting you

go.—   3. Now the   one thing   I   know that won't change.   'Cause it's

hard,   so — hard,   it's   tear - ing out   my   heart,—   it's—

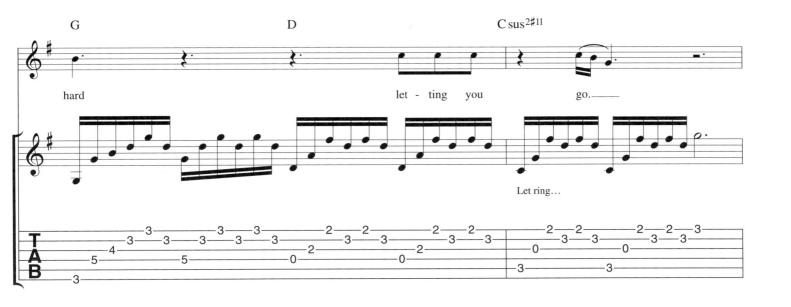

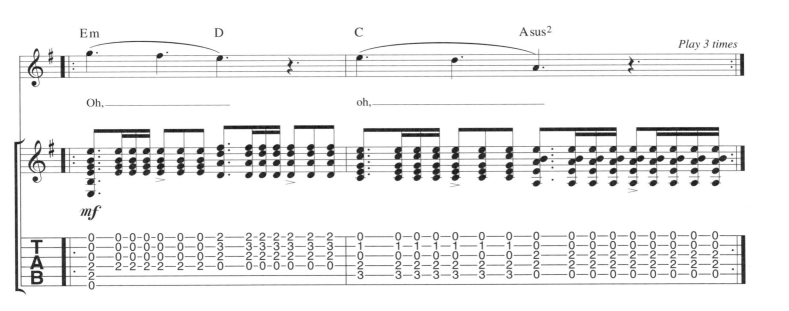

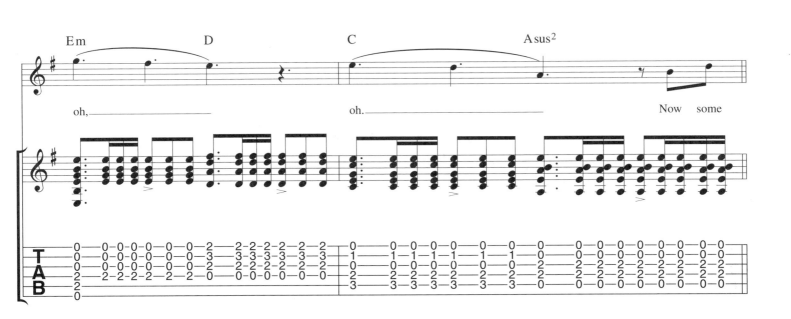

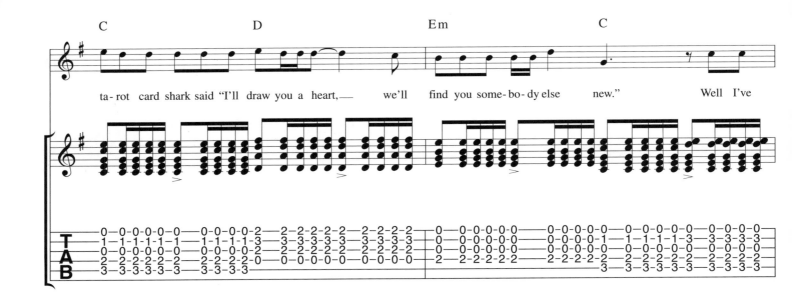

ta-rot card shark said "I'll draw you a heart,— we'll find you some-bo-dy else new." Well I've

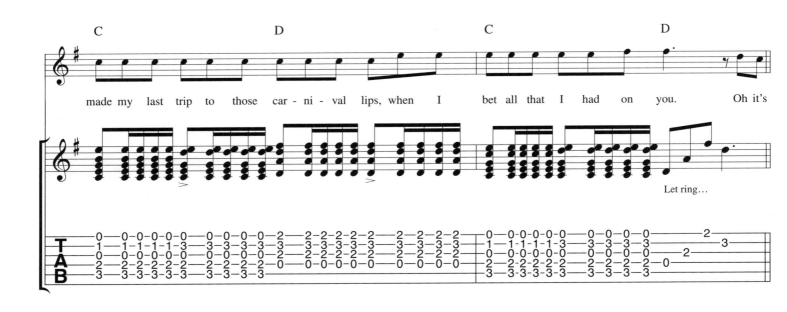

made my last trip to those car-ni-val lips, when I bet all that I had on you. Oh it's

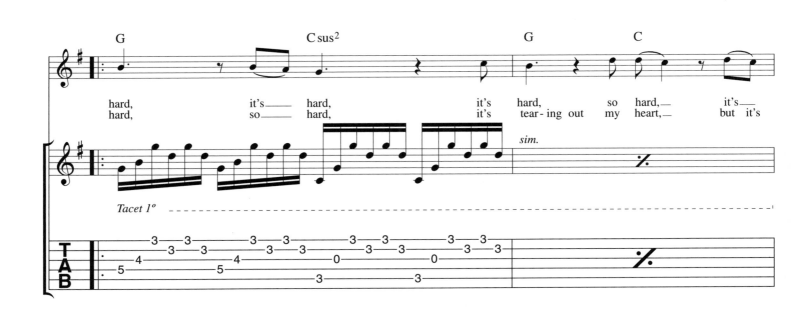

hard, it's—— hard, it's hard, so hard,— it's——
hard, so—— hard, it's tear-ing out my heart,— but it's

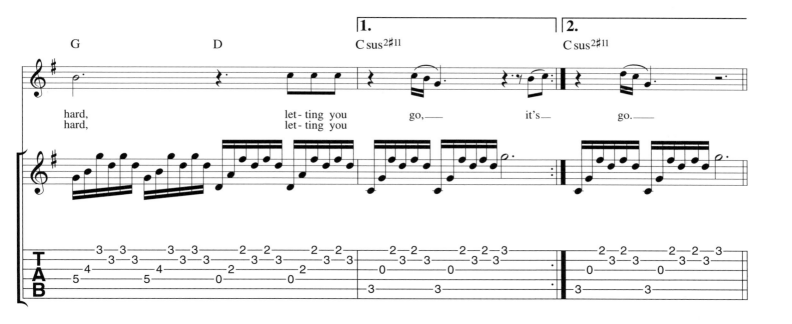

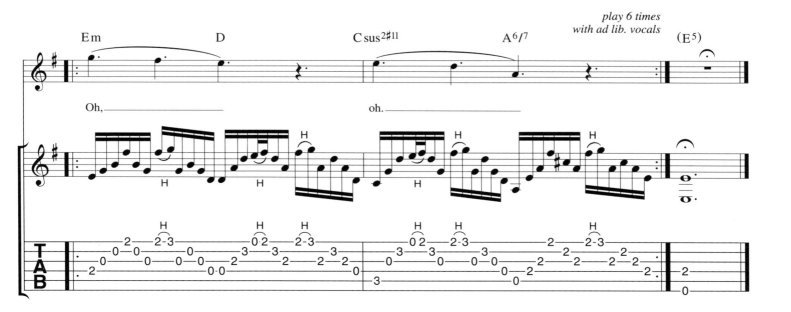

Verse 2:
I drove all night down streets that wouldn't bend
But somehow they drove me back here once again
To the place I lost at love, to the place that we called home
It would all have been so easy if you'd only made me cry
And told me how you're leaving me to some organ grinder's lullaby.

Verse 3:
Now the sky, it shines a different kind of blue
And the neighbour's dog don't bark like he used to
Well me - these days I just miss you; it's the nights I go insane
Unless you're coming back for me, I know one thing that won't change.

Hearts Breaking Even

Words & Music by Jon Bon Jovi & Desmond Child

1. It's a cold___ cold cold cold___ cold
(Verse 2 see block lyric)

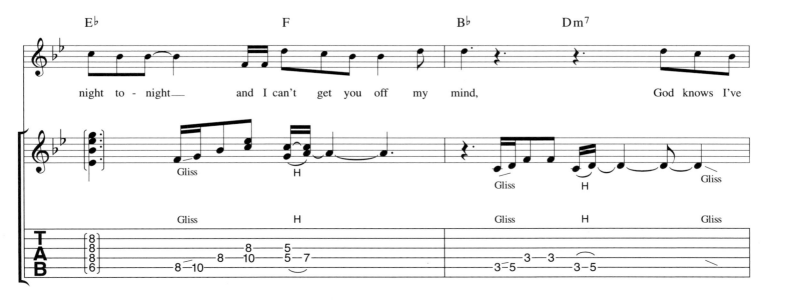

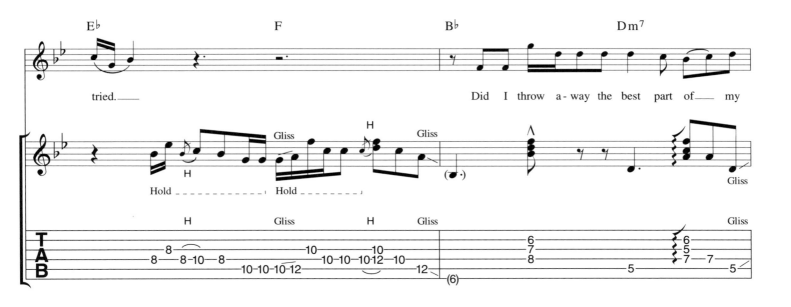

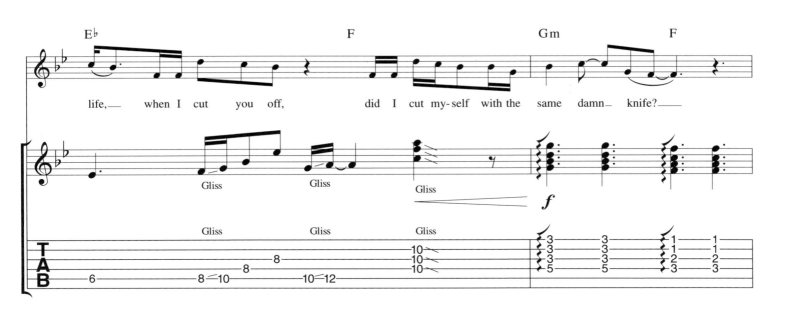

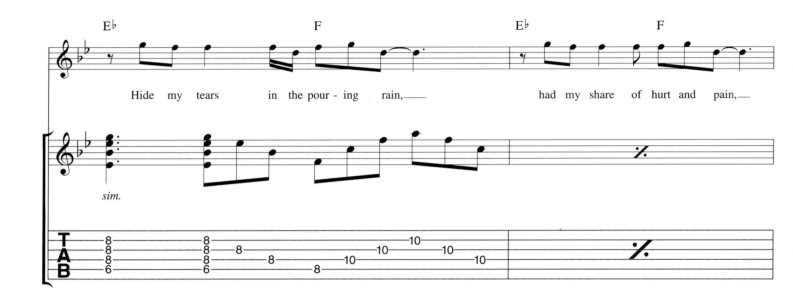

Hide my tears in the pour-ing rain,——— had my share of hurt and pain,———

don't say my name, run-a-way, 'cause it's all in

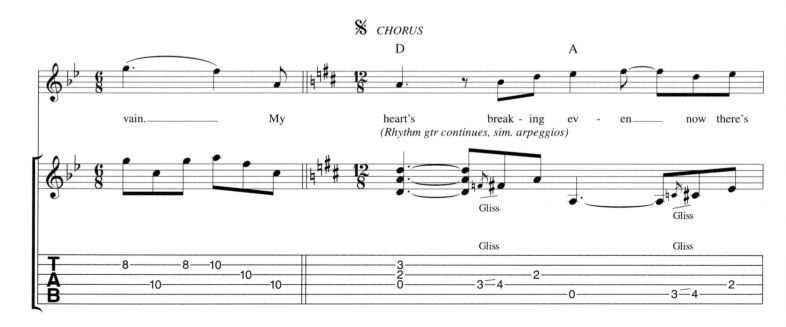

§ CHORUS

vain.————— My heart's break-ing ev-en——— now there's

(Rhythm gtr continues, sim. arpeggios)

94

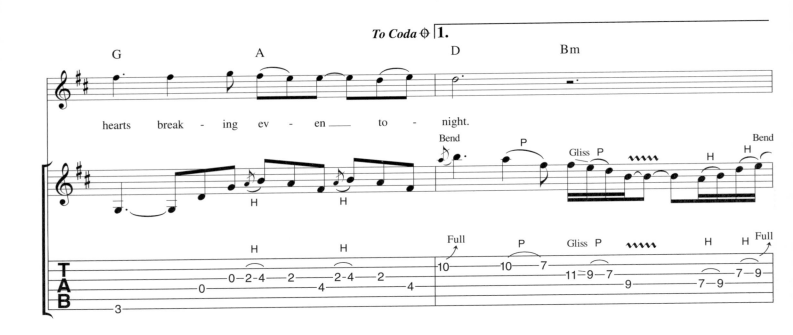

hearts break - ing ev - en —— to - night.

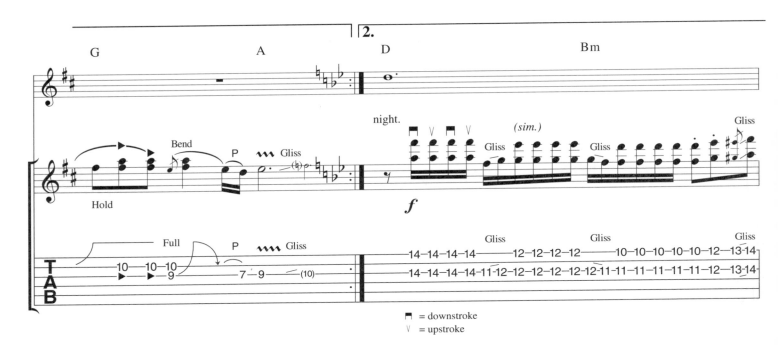

∏ = downstroke
V = upstroke

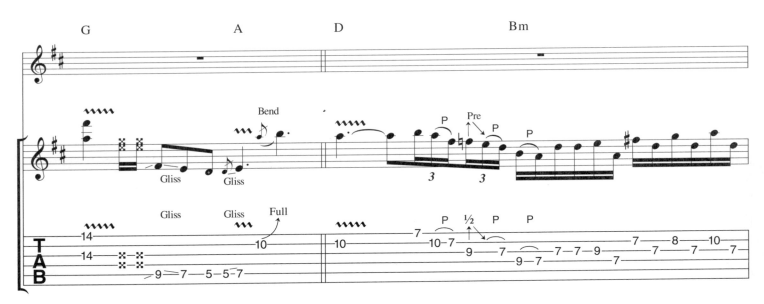

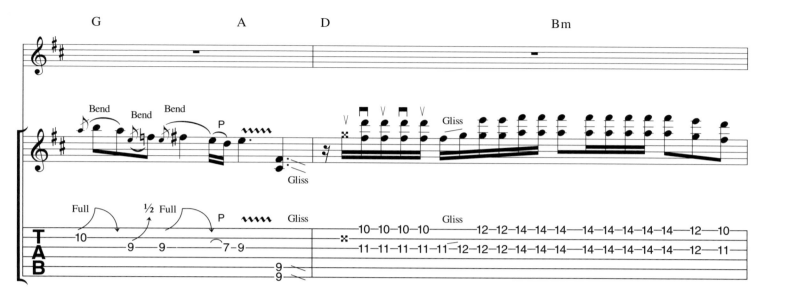

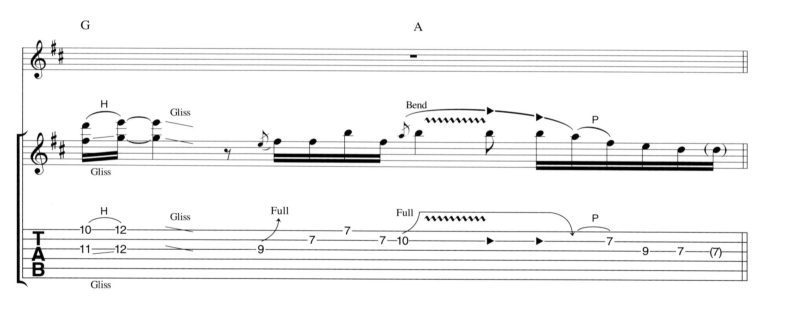

Go on, get on with your life,   yeah and I'll get on with mine,

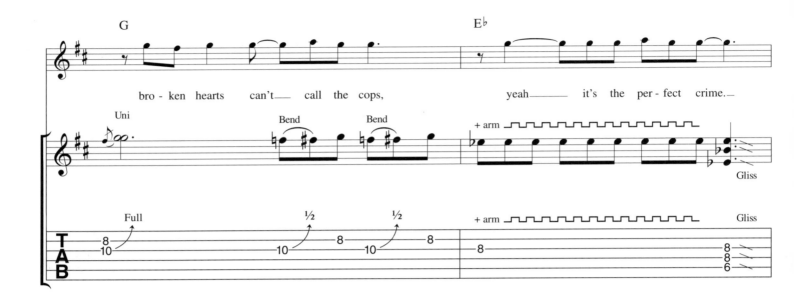

bro - ken hearts can't___ call the cops,   yeah___ it's the per - fect crime.___

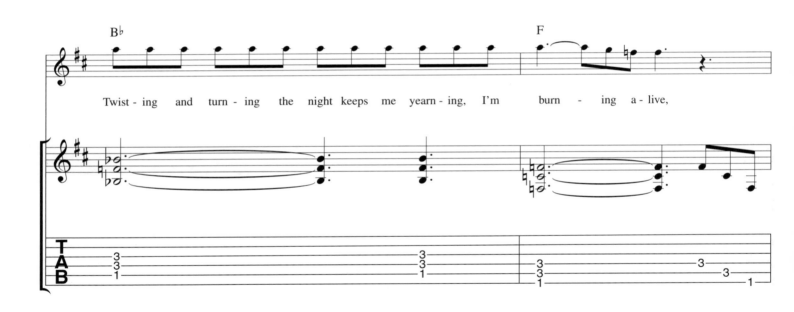

Twist - ing and turn - ing the night keeps me yearn - ing, I'm burn - ing a - live,

D.%. al Coda

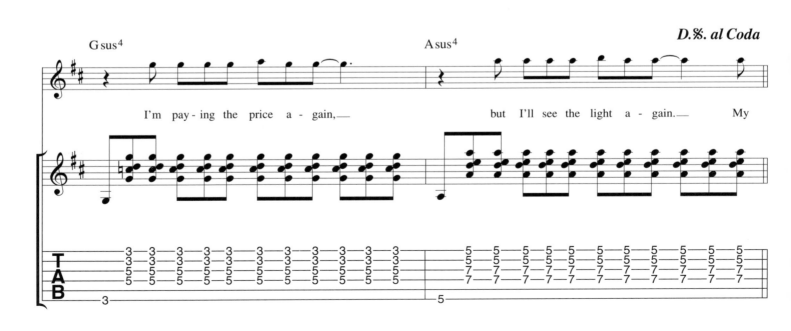

I'm pay - ing the price a - gain,___   but I'll see the light a - gain.___ My

Coda

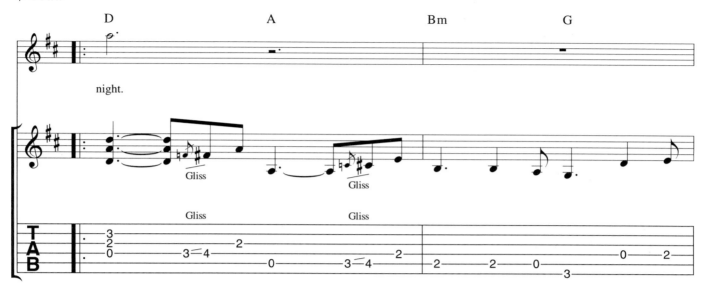

night.

Verse 2:
It's been a long long long long long time
Since I had your love here in my hands
We didn't understand it, we couldn't understand it
But nothing's fair in love and hate
You lay it all down and walk away before it's too late
We danced all night as the music played
The sheets got tangled in the mess we made
There in the stains we remain
No one left to blame.

Something To Believe In

Words & Music by Jon Bon Jovi

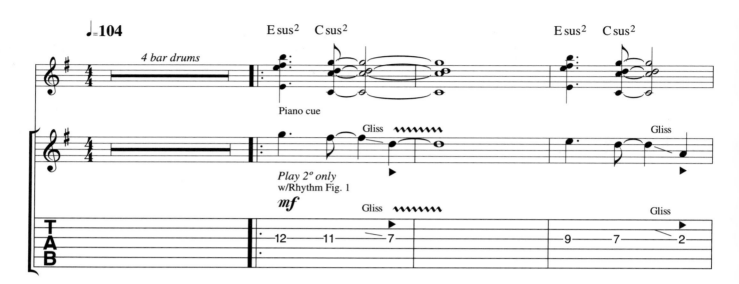

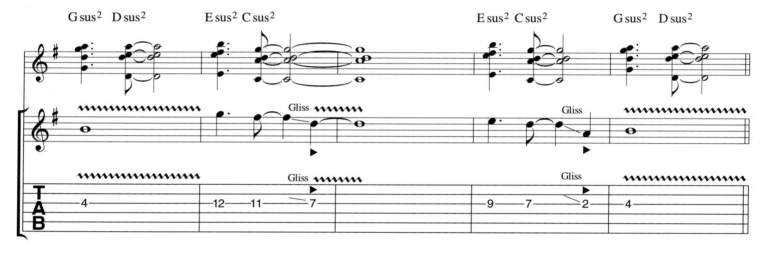

VERSE

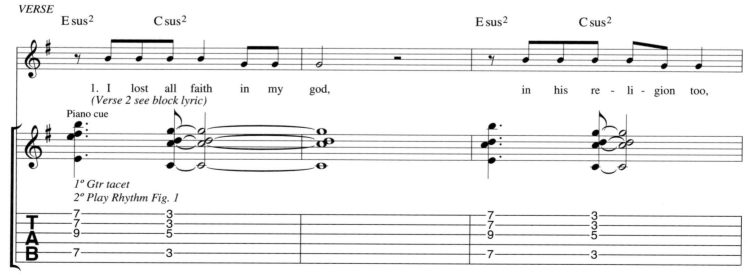

1. I lost all faith in my god, in his re-li-gion too,
(Verse 2 see block lyric)

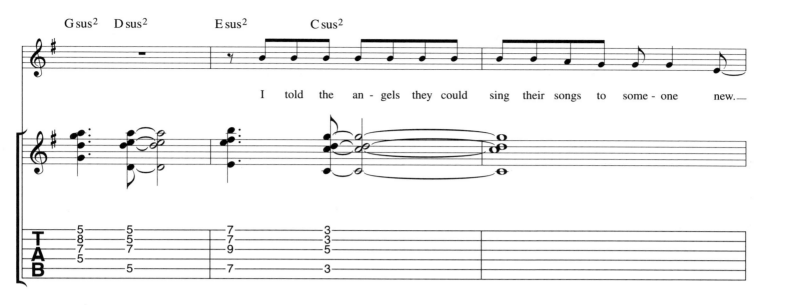

I told the an-gels they could sing their songs to some-one new.

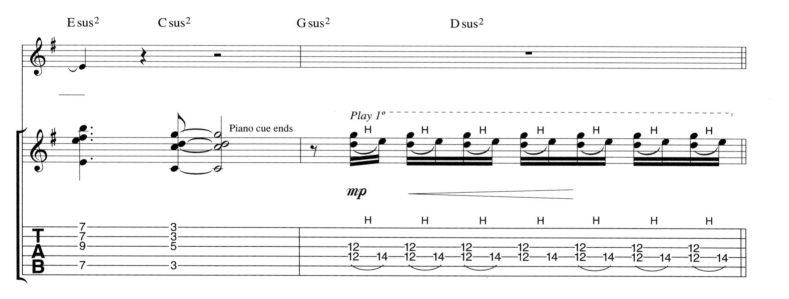

Piano cue ends

Play 1°

mp

I lost all trust in my——— friends,

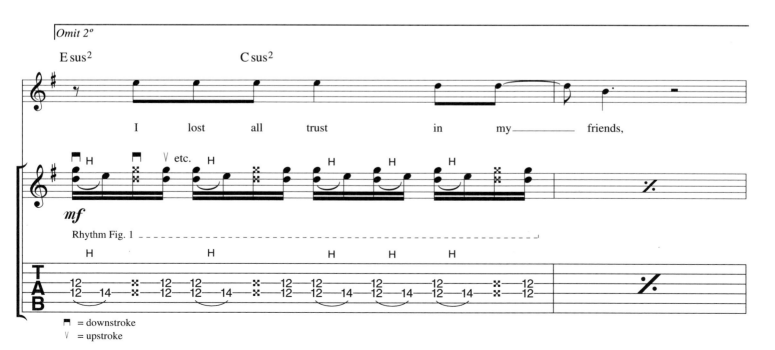

Rhythm Fig. 1

⊓ = downstroke

V = upstroke

I watched my heart turn to stone,

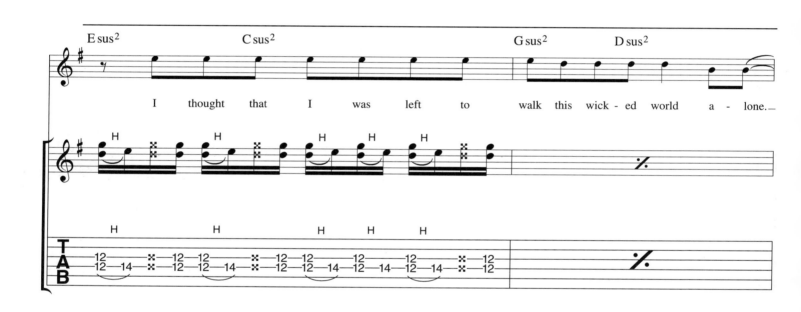

I thought that I was left to walk this wick - ed world a - lone.

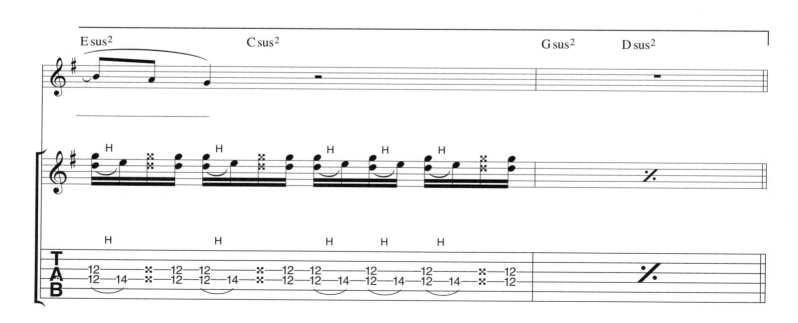

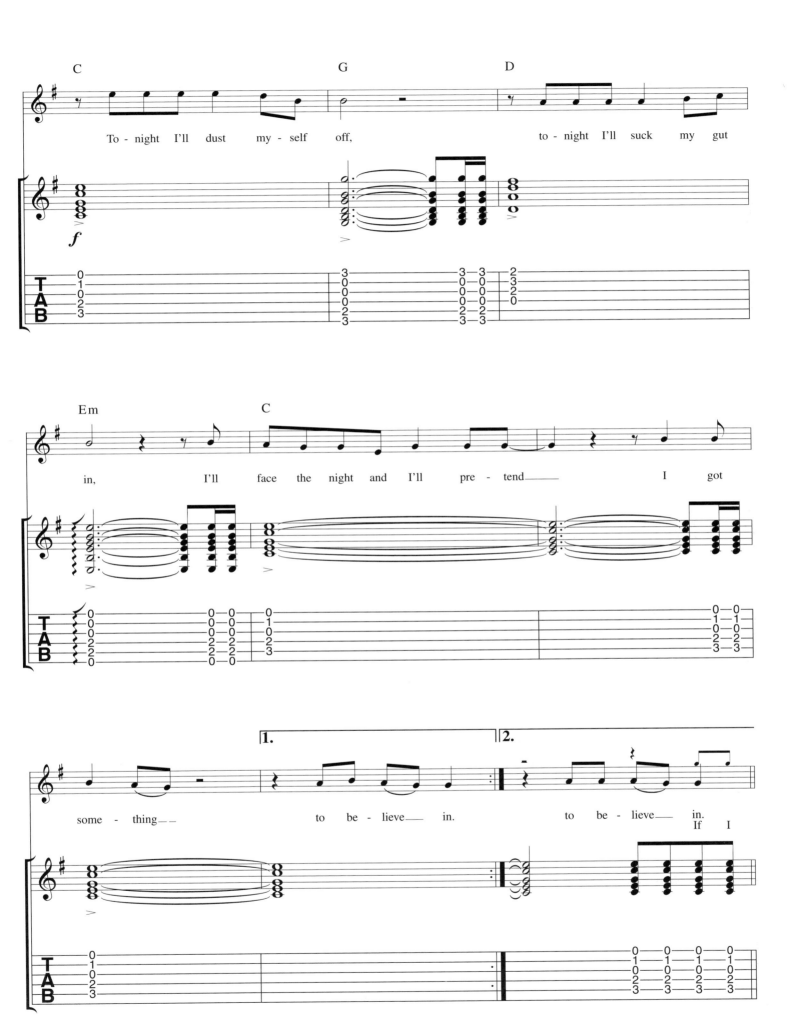

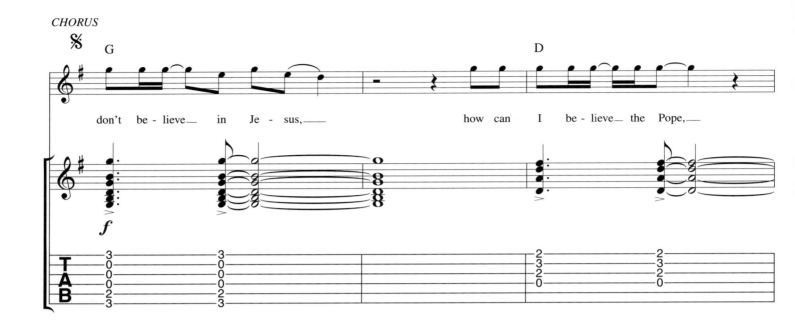

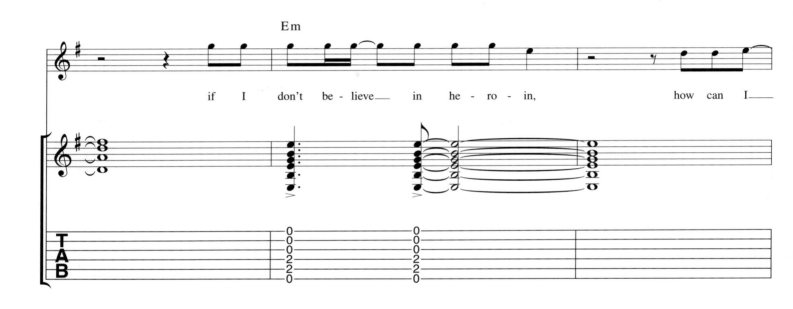

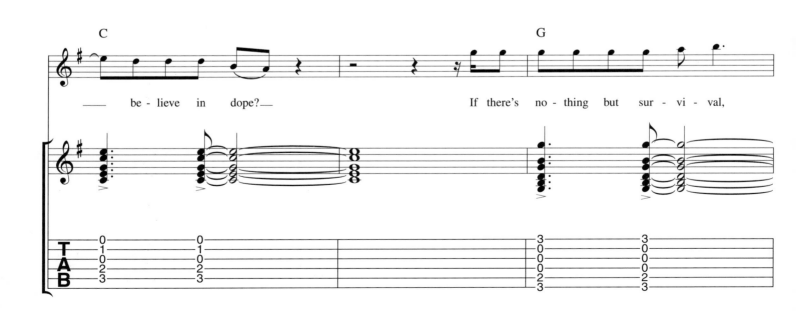

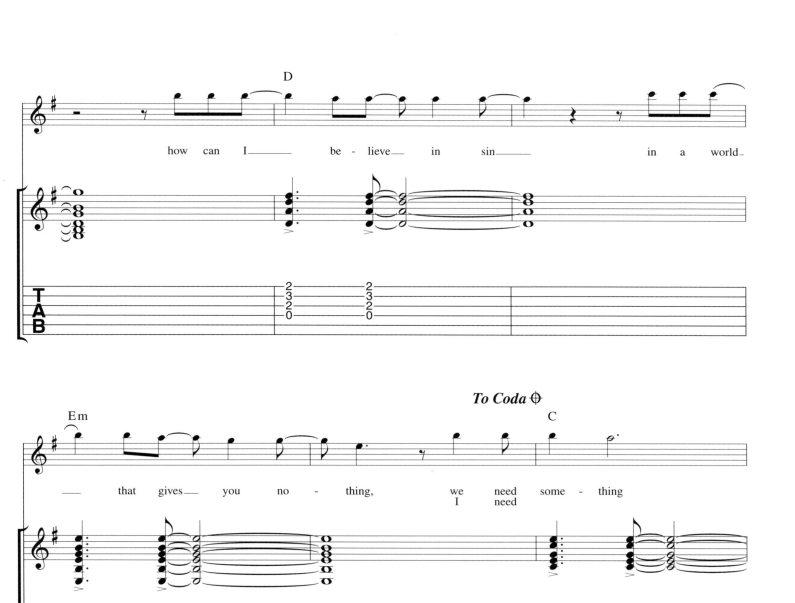

how can I ____ be - lieve ____ in sin ____ in a world ____

To Coda ⊕

that gives ____ you no - thing, we need some - thing
I need

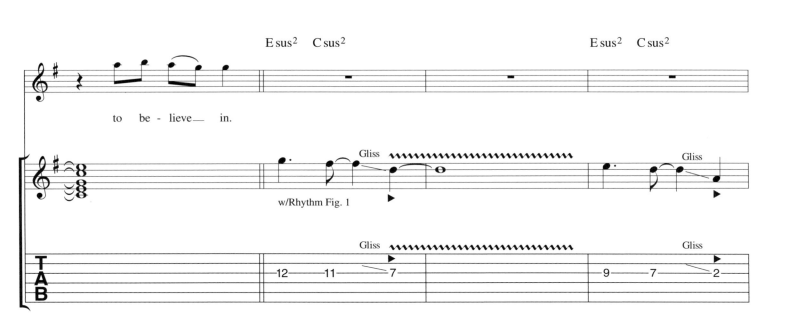

to be - lieve ____ in.

w/Rhythm Fig. 1

Some - thing to be - lieve___ in.

Some - thing to be - lieve___ in. _____

Rhythm Break

Gliss

Bend

1/2   + hold -

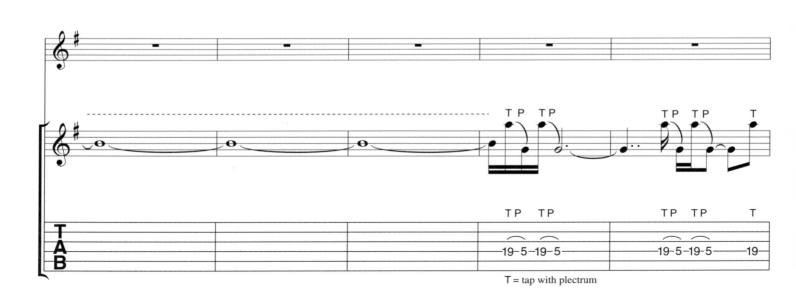

T = tap with plectrum

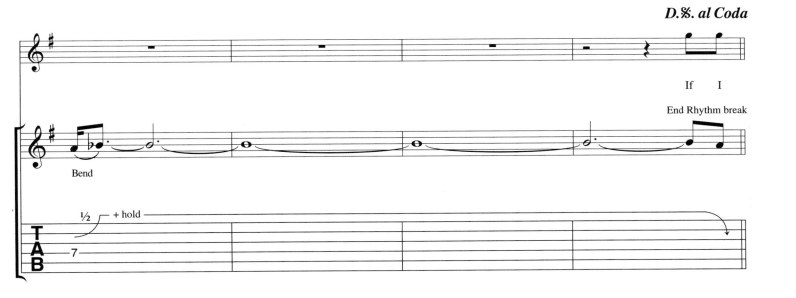

Coda

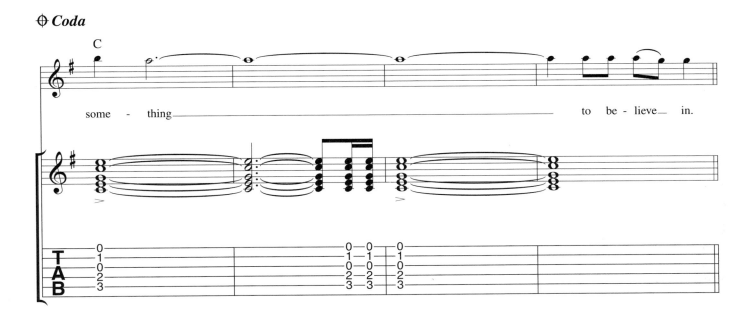

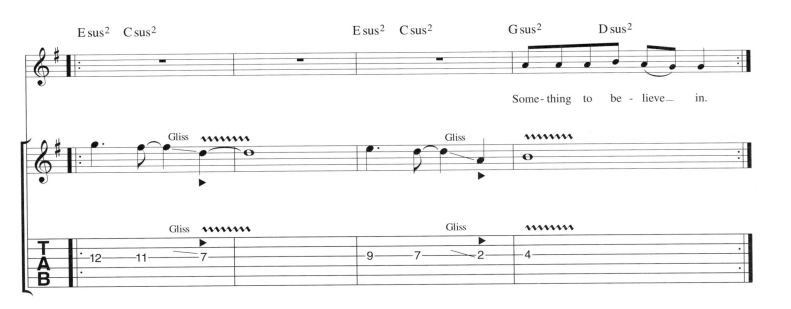

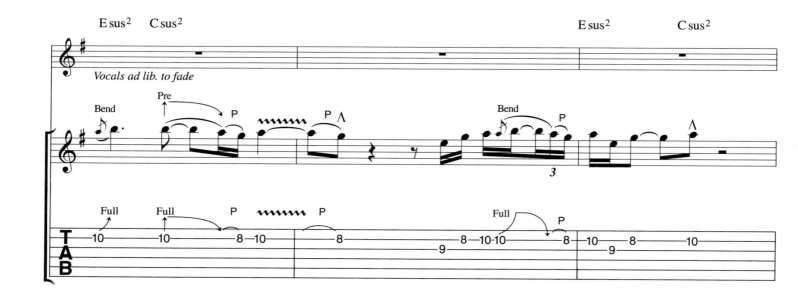

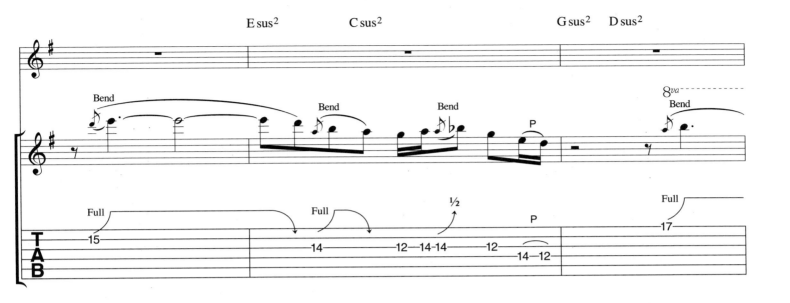

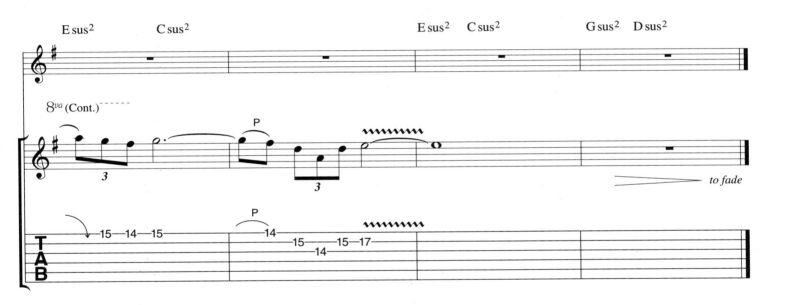

Verse 2:
And I had lost touch with reason
I watched life criticise the truth
Been waiting for a miracle
I know you have too.

Though I know I won't win
I'll take this one on the chin
We'll raise a toast and I'll pretend
I got something to believe in.

If That's What It Takes

Words & Music by Jon Bon Jovi & Richie Sambora

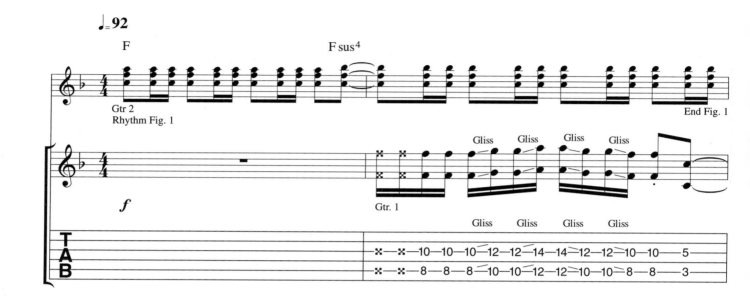

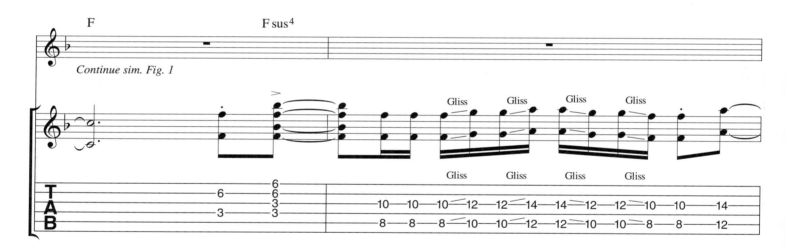

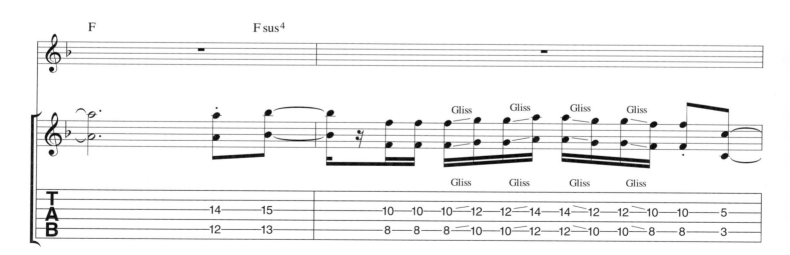

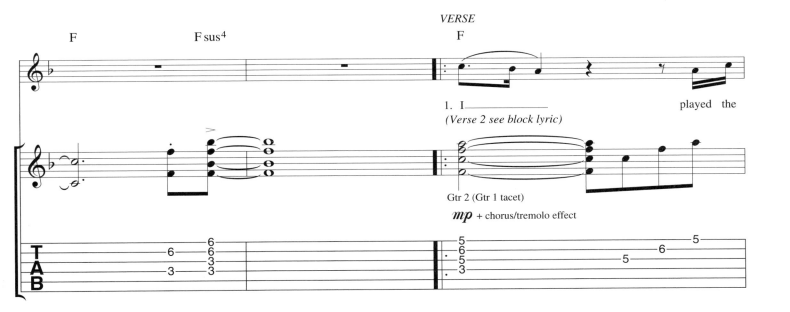

VERSE

1. I_____

(Verse 2 see block lyric)

played the

Gtr 2 (Gtr 1 tacet)

mp + chorus/tremolo effect

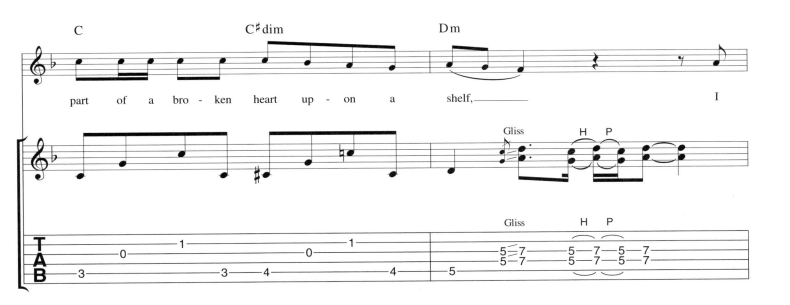

part of a bro-ken heart up-on a shelf,_____ I

Gliss   H   P

played that part so lone-ly and so well,_____

Let ring…

sim.

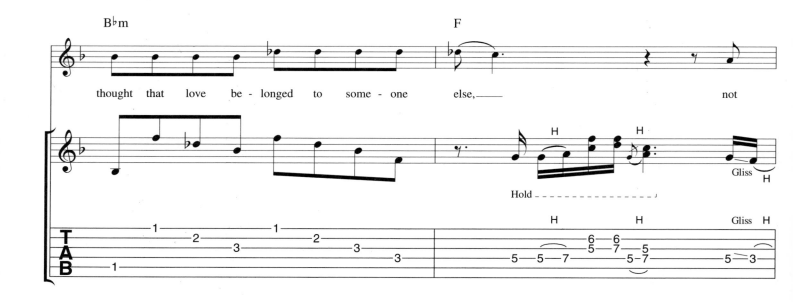

thought that love be-longed to some-one else,_____ not

me and you. Yeah,_____ I know that you've been shat-tered, you've been

bruised,__ and we both know what it feels like when we lose,_____ but I'd

bet my life on a roll of the dice___ for you.___

§ *CHORUS*

If that's what it takes___ that's what I'd do,___ to - night's the night___

◻ = downstroke

∨ = upstroke

___ I'm gon - na prove it to you.___ Do I have to break down___ ba - by just to break through?___

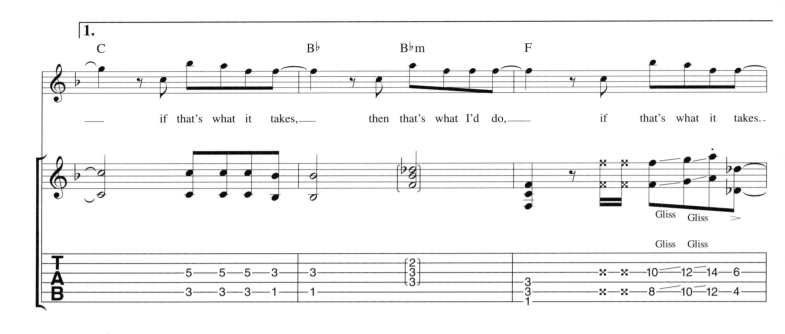

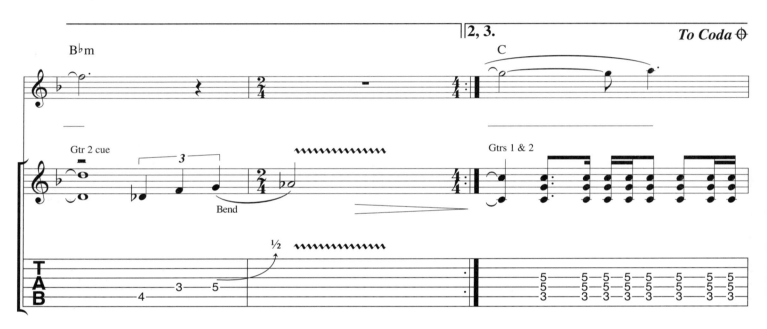

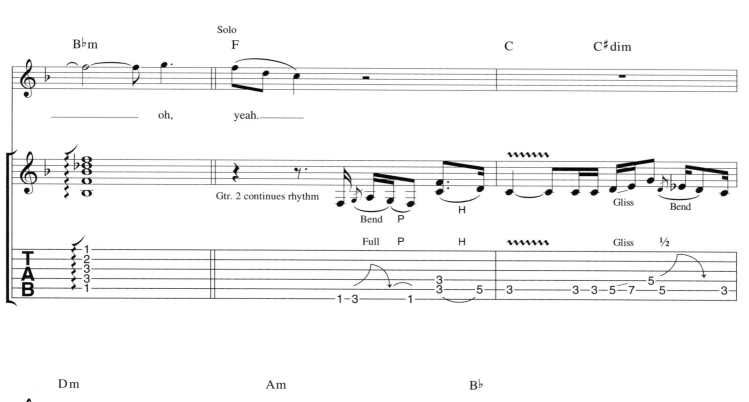

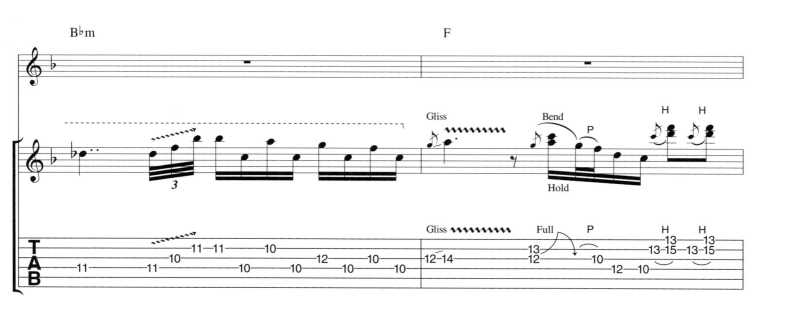

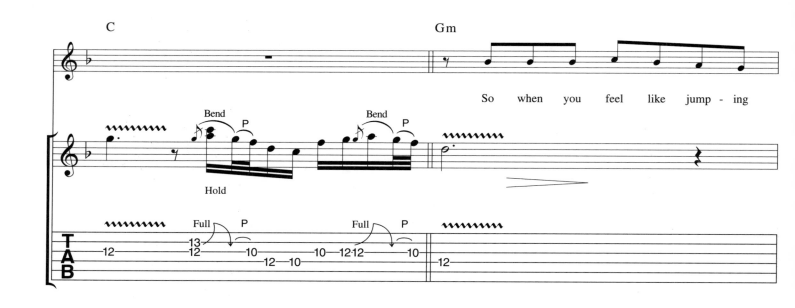

So when you feel like jump - ing

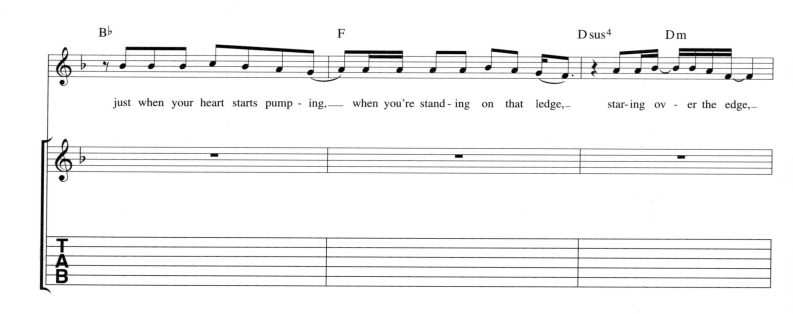

just when your heart starts pump - ing,— when you're stand - ing on that ledge,— star - ing ov - er the edge,—

I'll be there— to talk you down,— I'll be there be - fore you hit the ground.—

Gtrs 1 & 2

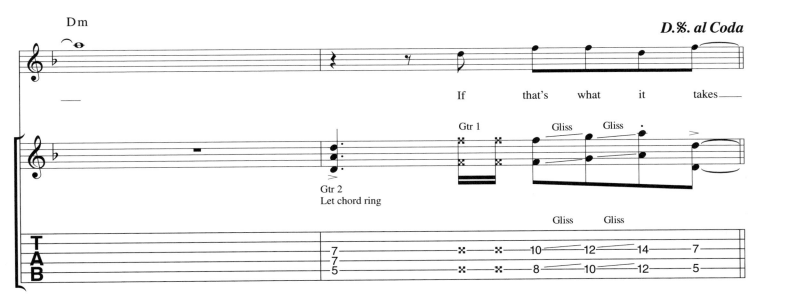

D.%. al Coda

If that's what it takes

Gtr 1

Gliss Gliss

Gtr 2
Let chord ring

Gliss Gliss

⊕ *Coda*

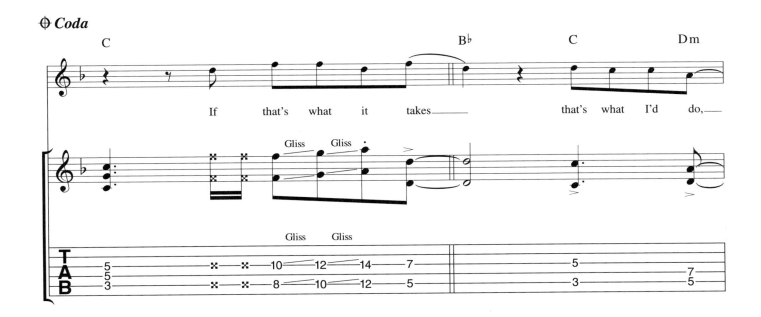

C   B♭   C   Dm

If that's what it takes_____   that's what I'd do,____

Gliss Gliss

Gliss Gliss

B♭

____ if we take the time to get it right_____   I know we'll pull through,—

Gliss Gliss

Gliss Gliss

Gliss

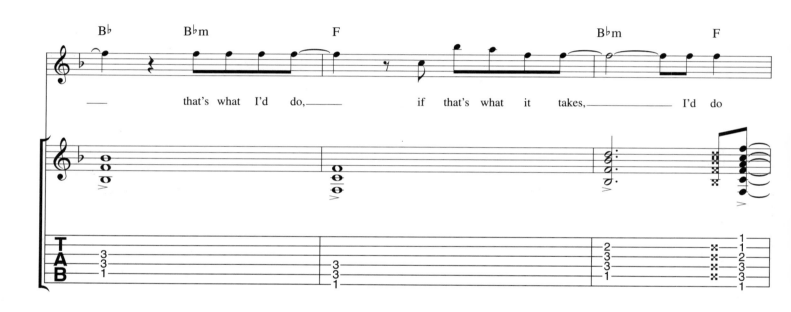

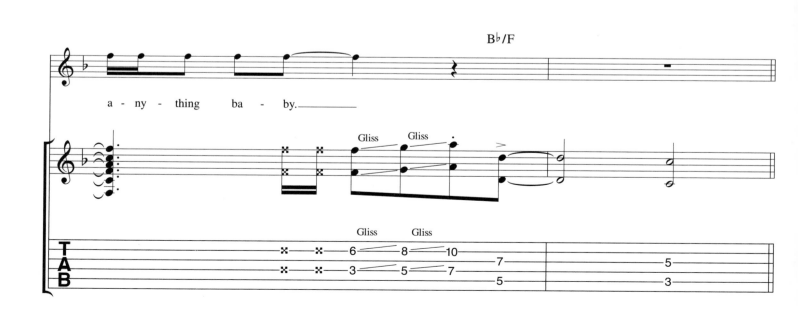

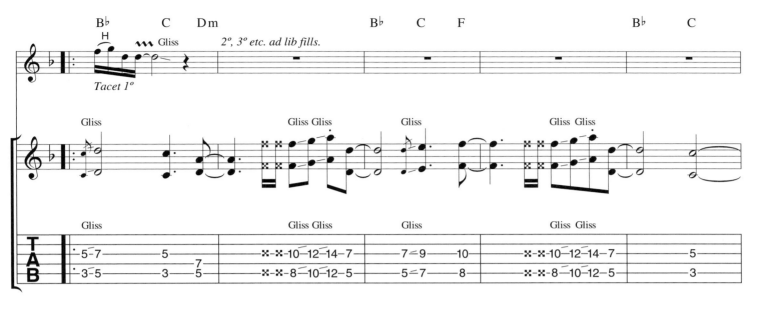

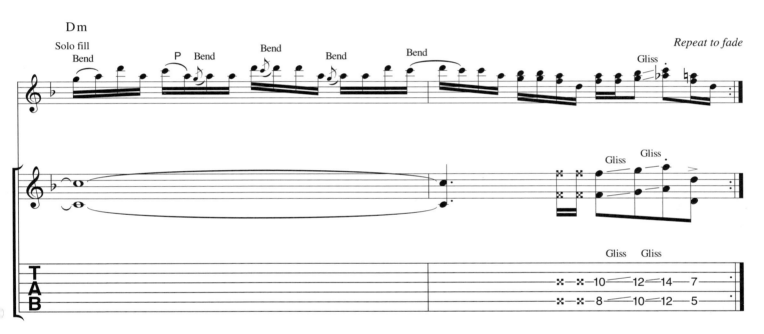

Verse 2:
I bet you counted all the tears, I bet you cried
I bet you swore you'd never let love back inside
'Cause it hurt you way too bad to say goodbye.
Now there'll be times when I might put us to the test
And it's hard for broken hearts to just forget
But I'm driving blind, I'll lay it all on the line for you.

Diamond Ring

Words & Music by Jon Bon Jovi, Richie Sambora & Desmond Child

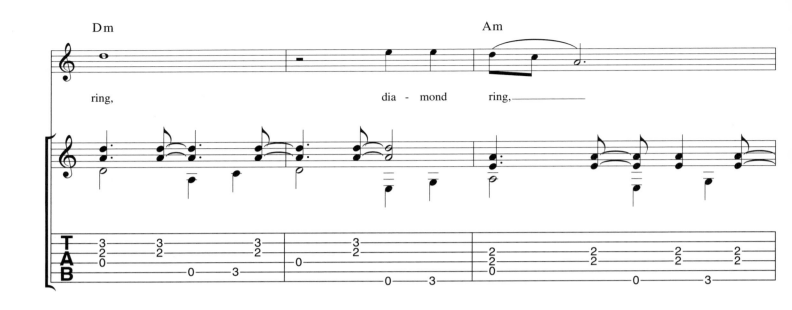

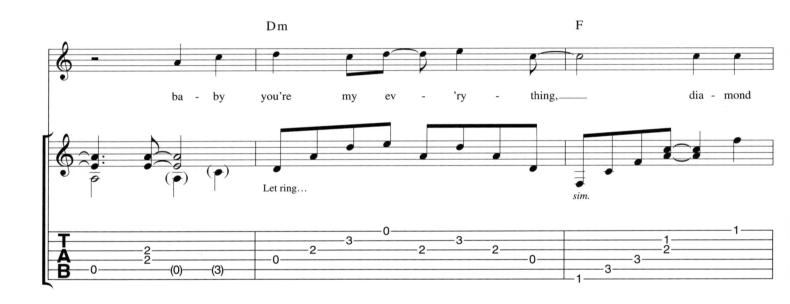

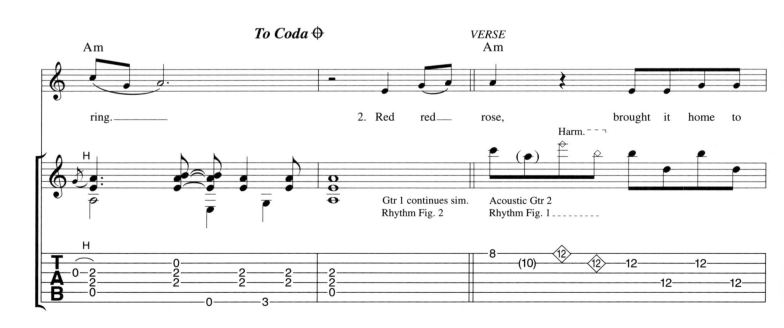

you,   blood red— rose   tells me that you're true.   Red,   red

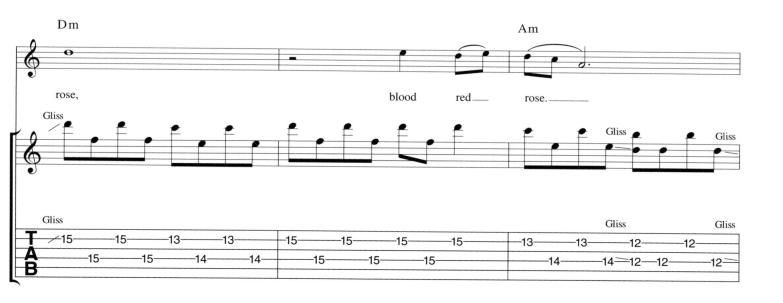

rose,   blood red— rose.———

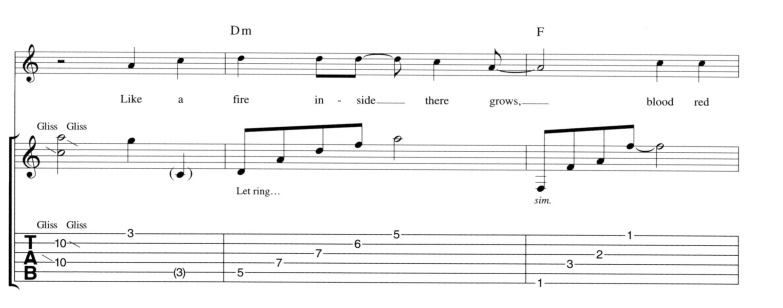

Like   a   fire   in - side—— there   grows,——   blood red

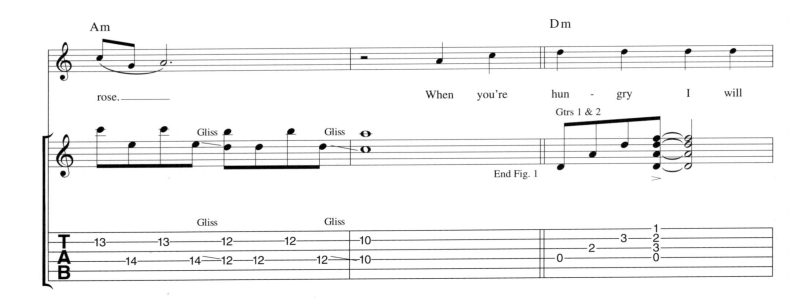

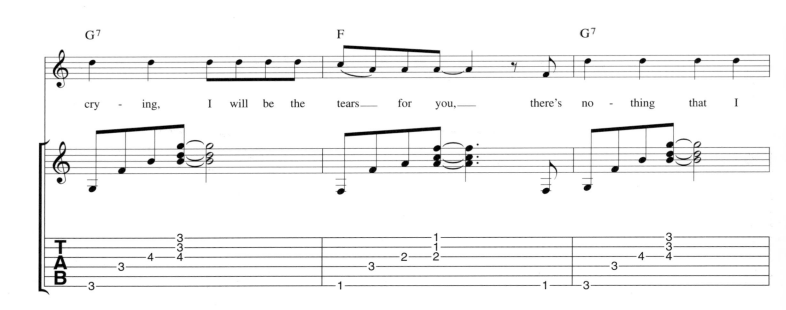

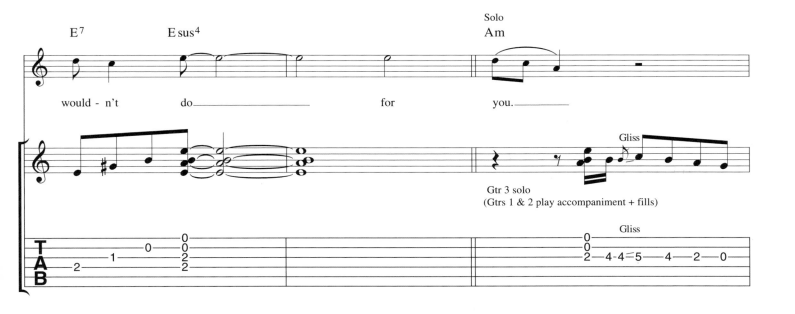

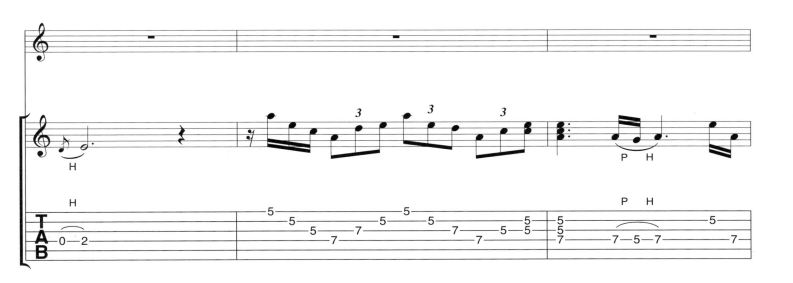

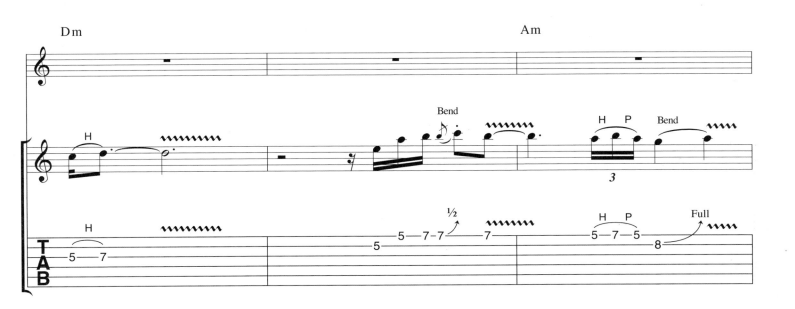

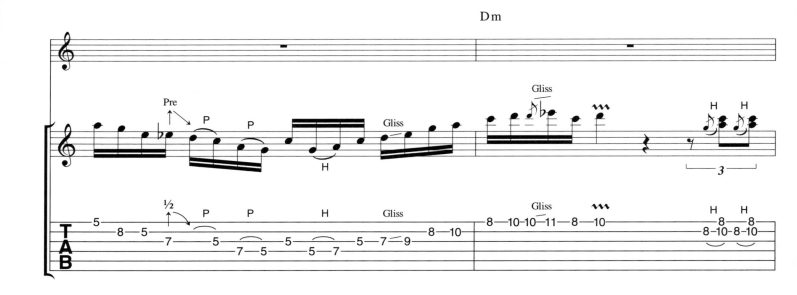

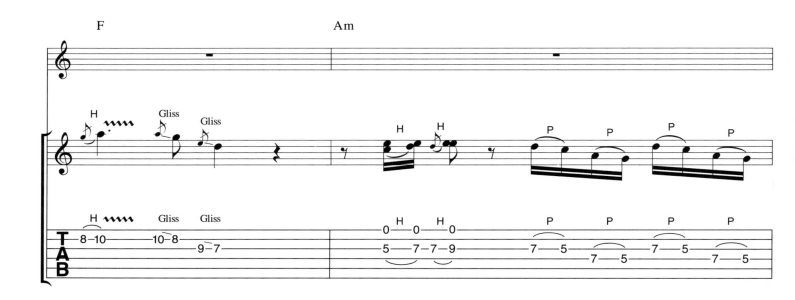

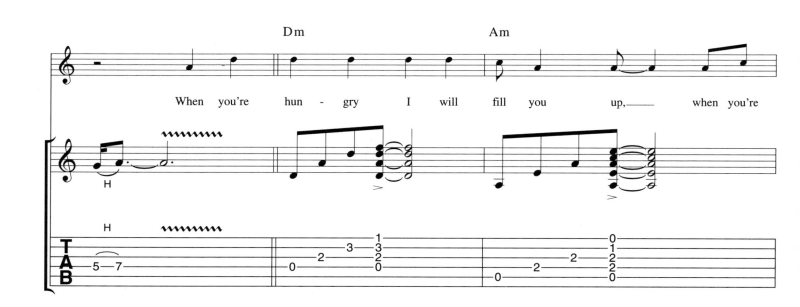

When you're hun - gry I will fill you up,——— when you're

thir - sty, drink out of my —— lov - ing cup, —— when you're cry - ing, I will be the

tears —— for you, —— there's no - thing that I would - n't do. ——

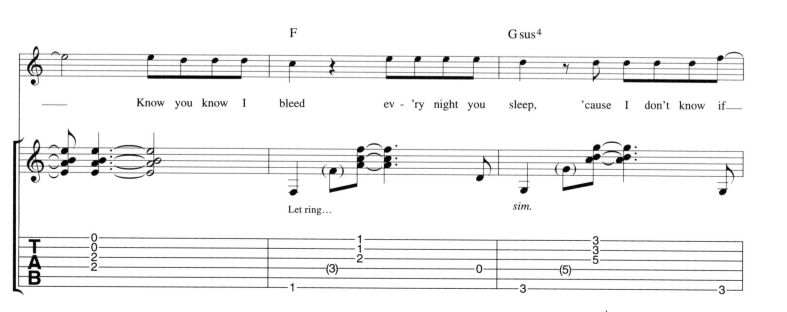

—— Know you know I bleed ev -'ry night you sleep, 'cause I don't know if ——

Let ring…   sim.

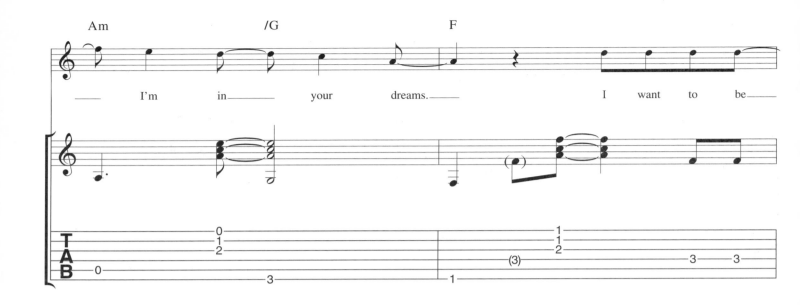

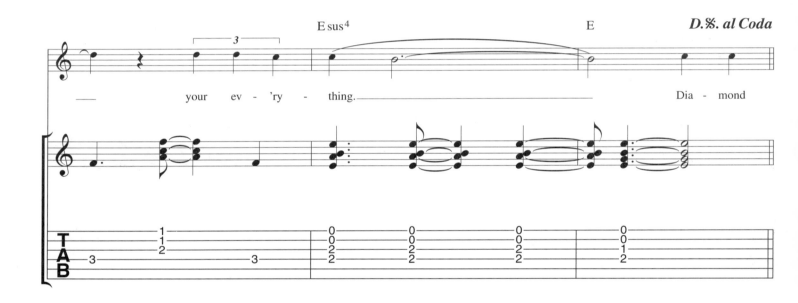

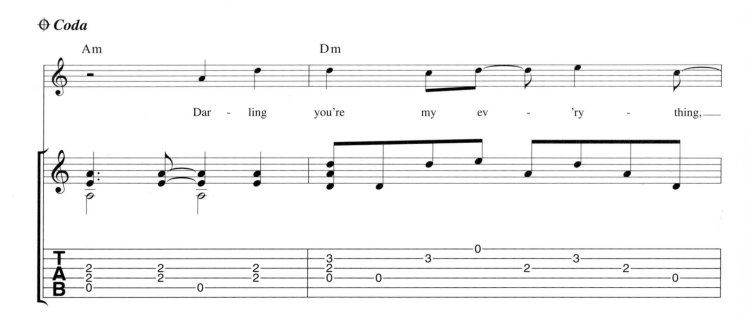

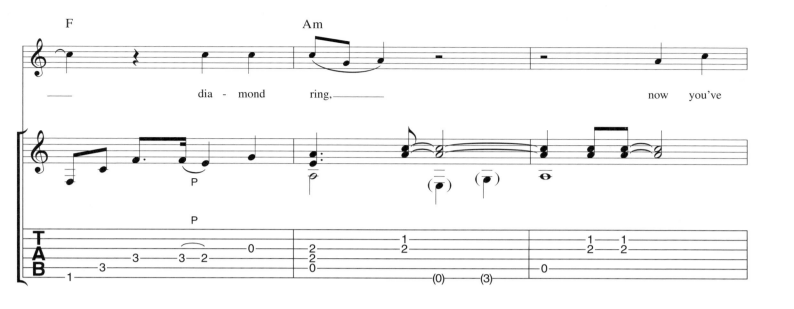

dia - mond   ring,_____   now you've

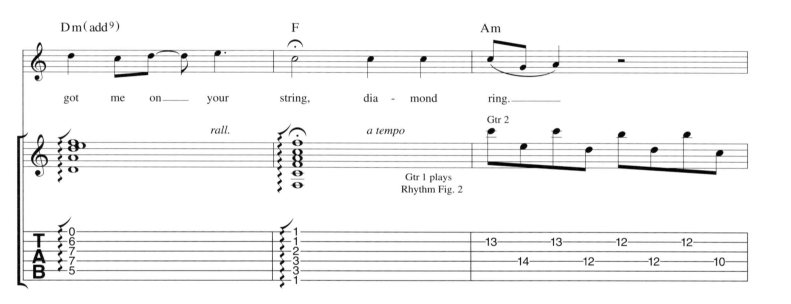

got   me   on____   your   string,   dia - mond   ring.____

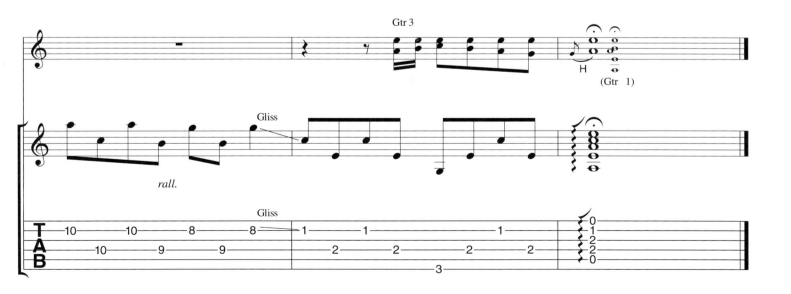

All I Want Is Everything

Words & Music by Jon Bon Jovi & Richie Sambora

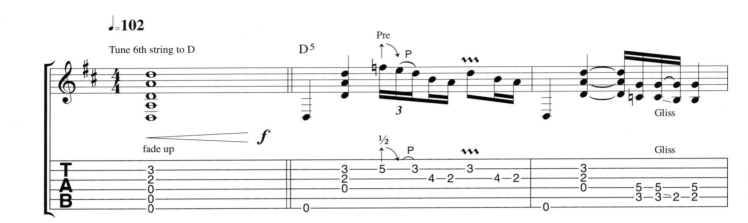

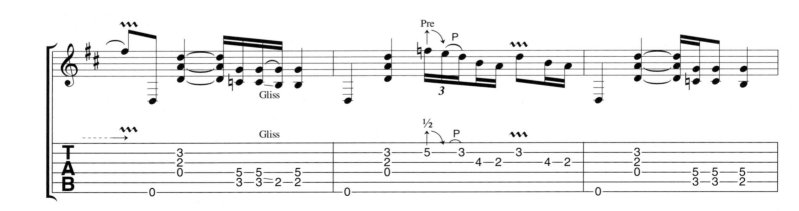

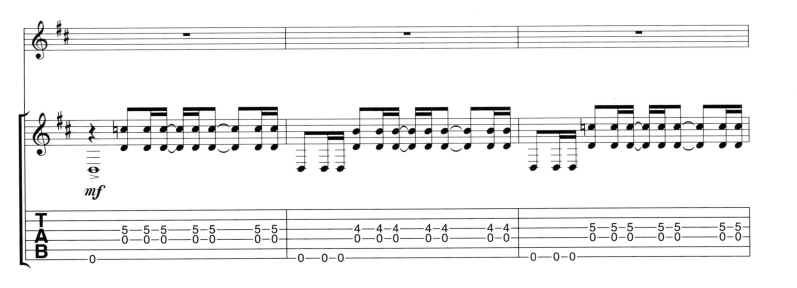

%

D⁵

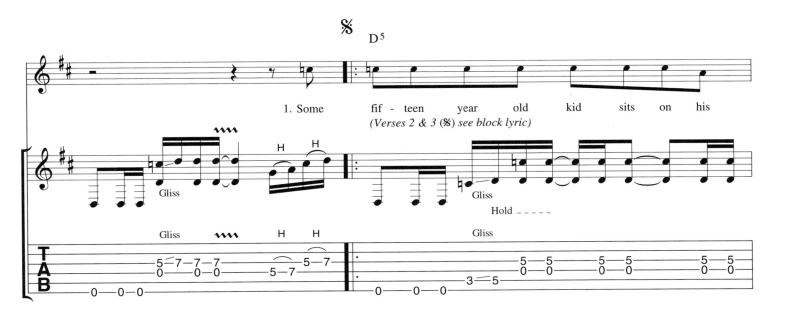

1. Some fif - teen year old kid sits on his
(Verses 2 & 3 (%) see block lyric)

porch just half - past noon, tryin' to fi - gure out just what he's do - ing, why he

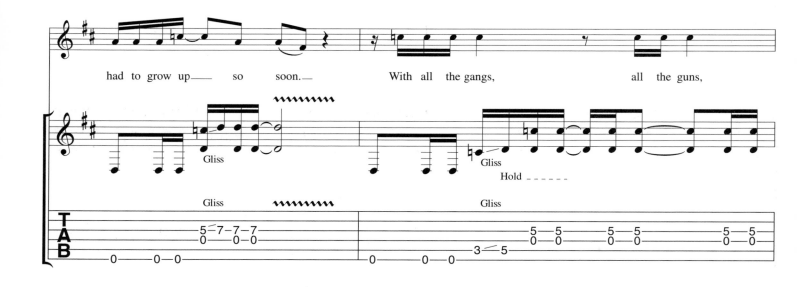

had to grow up— so soon.— With all the gangs, all the guns,

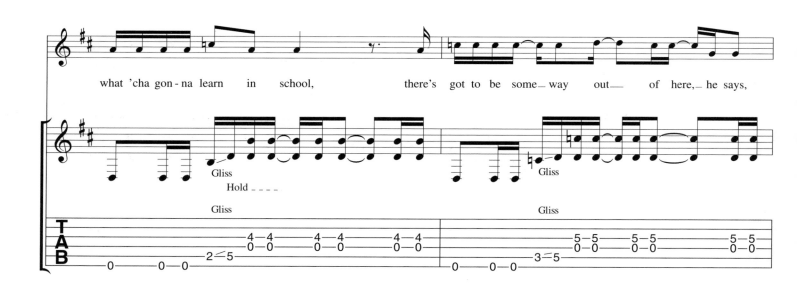

what 'cha gon - na learn in school, there's got to be some— way out— of here,— he says,

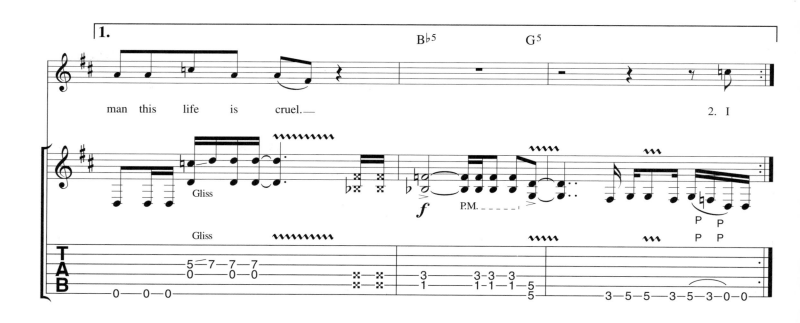

1.

Bb5 G5

man this life is cruel.— 2. I

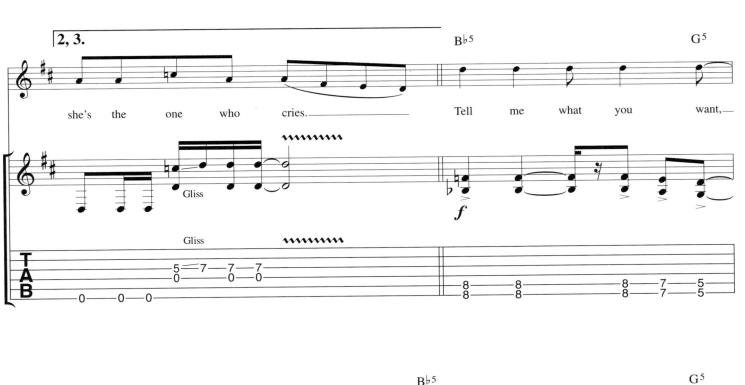

she's the one who cries._____ Tell me what you want,___

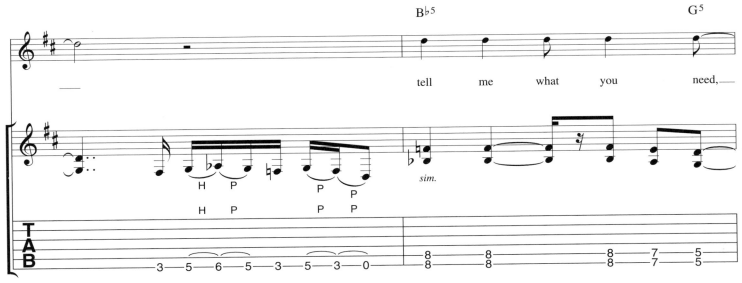

tell me what you need,___

I want ev - 'ry - thing._____ I've

I want more than I   see   com - in',   all   I   want   is   ev - 'ry - thing,—

all   I   want   is   ev -   'ry -   thing.

D.%. al Coda

$\oplus$ **Coda**

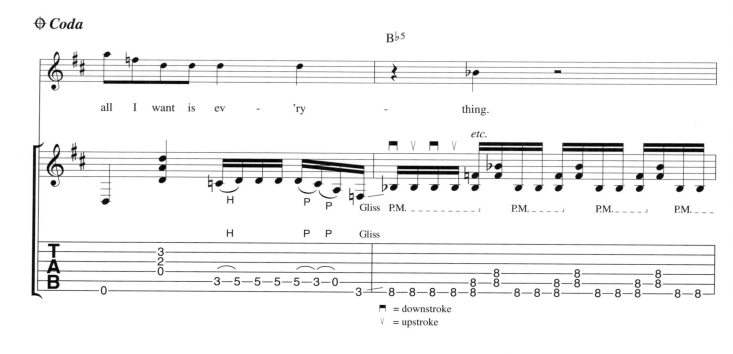

all I want is ev - 'ry - thing.

◼ = downstroke
∨ = upstroke

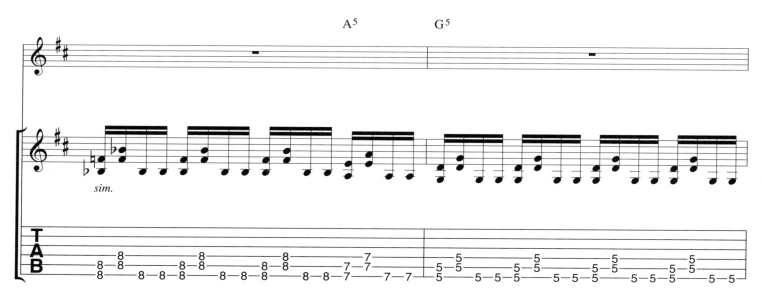

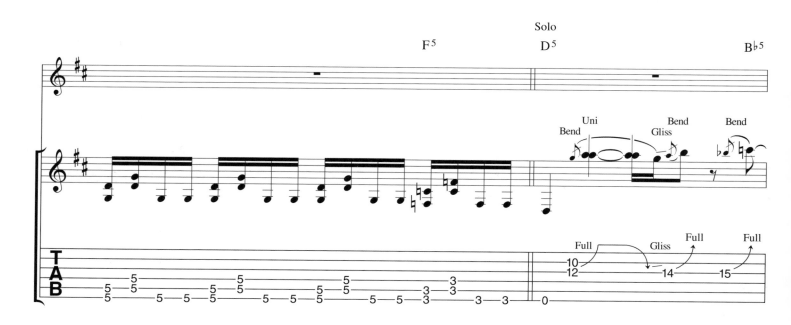

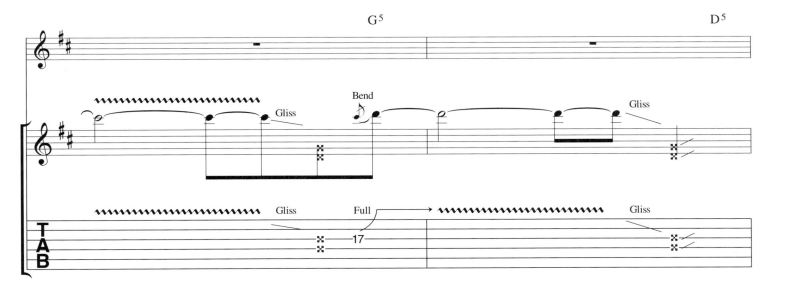

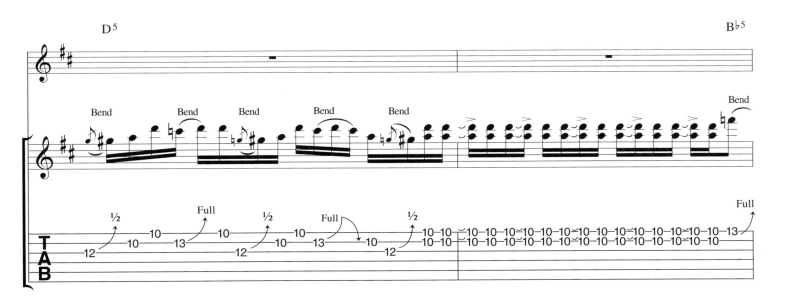

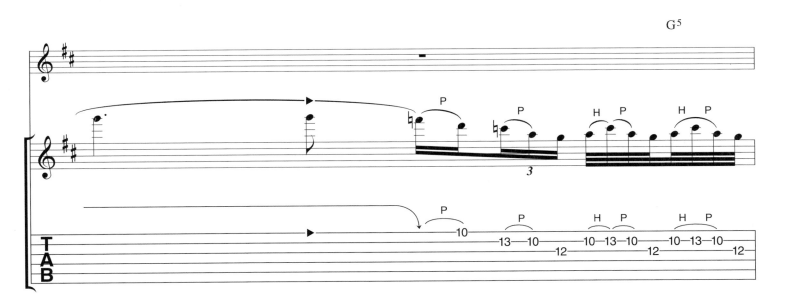

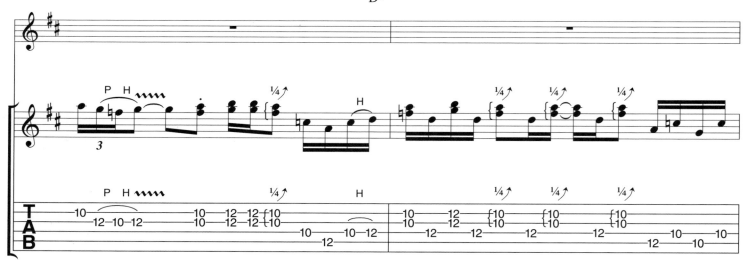

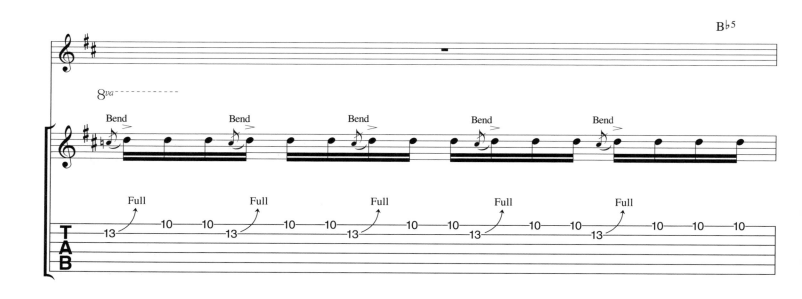

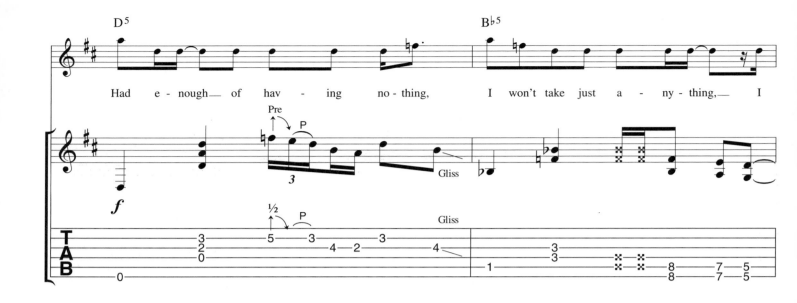

Had e - nough___ of hav - ing no - thing, I won't take just a - ny - thing,___ I

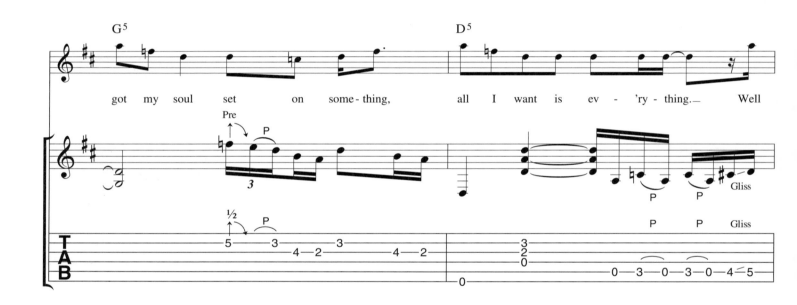

got my soul set on some - thing, all I want is ev - 'ry - thing.___ Well

it's my life mis - ter, I ain't run - nin', I'm no pup - pet on___ a string,

I want more than I see com - in', all I want is ev - 'ry - thing.

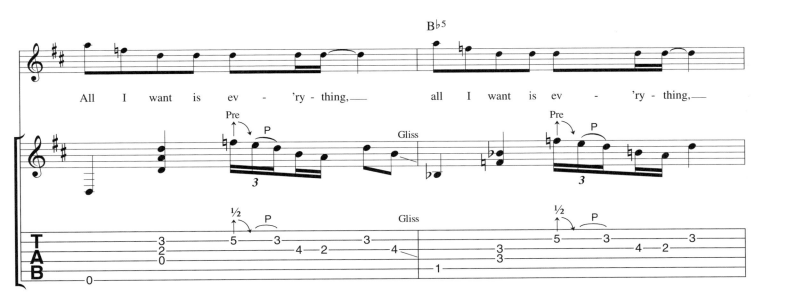

All I want is ev - 'ry - thing, all I want is ev - 'ry - thing,

all I want well, I want it all.

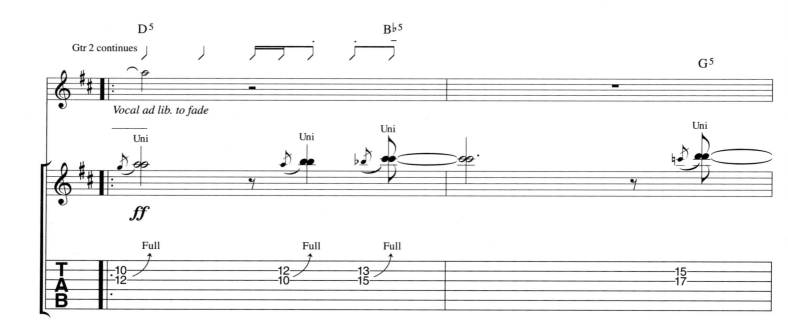

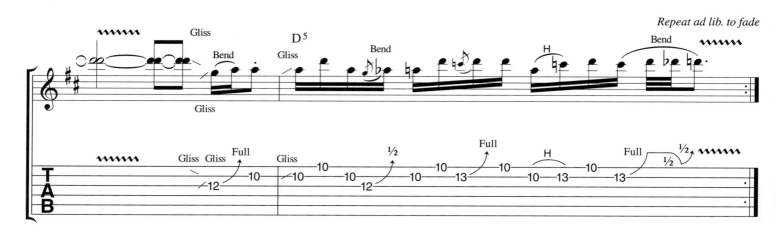

Verse 2:
I used to know this Puerto Rican girl who lied to change her life
She changed her name, her face
Because the grass looked greener on the other side
She turned her back, she ran away straight into the night
Her friends, her family feel the pain but she's the one who cries.

Verse 3 (%):
Say a prayer for Donnie, he died in his room just the other day
His brother come home, found him dead on the floor
With a needle in his vein
The cops come down with a body bag, they said, "Donnie's a casualty"
I said, "All it's about is the boy checked out, he couldn't handle reality."

Bitter Wine

Words & Music by Jon Bon Jovi & Richie Sambora

1. We met some time a-go,——— when we were al-most young,—
(Verse 2 see block lyric)

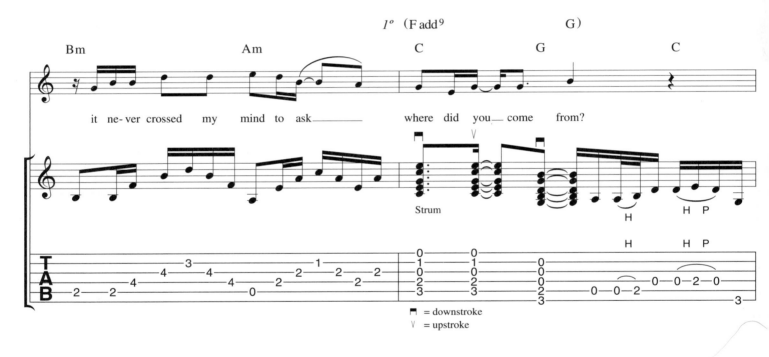

it ne-ver crossed my mind to ask——— where did you—— come from?

◻ = downstroke
V = upstroke

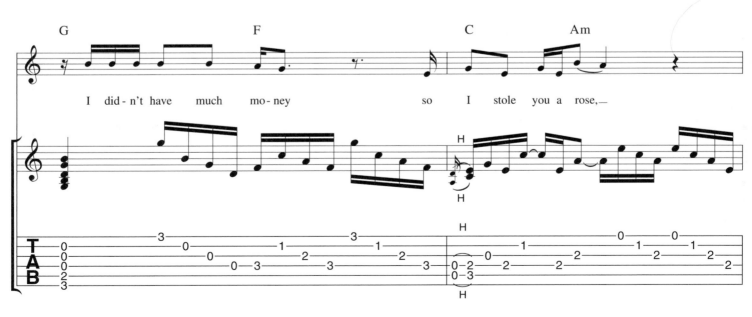

I did-n't have much mo-ney so I stole you a rose,—

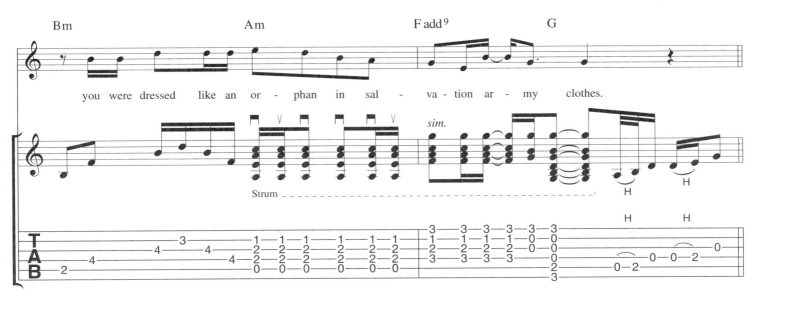

you were dressed like an or - phan in sal - va - tion ar - my clothes.

I ne - ver thought I'd lose you,— no I'd ra - ther go— blind,—

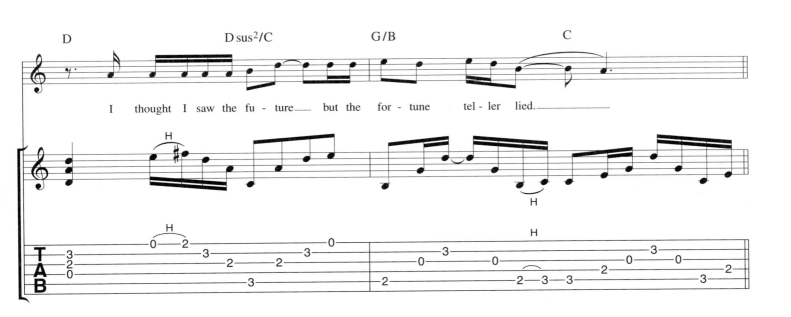

I thought I saw the fu - ture— but the for - tune tel - ler lied.——

CHORUS

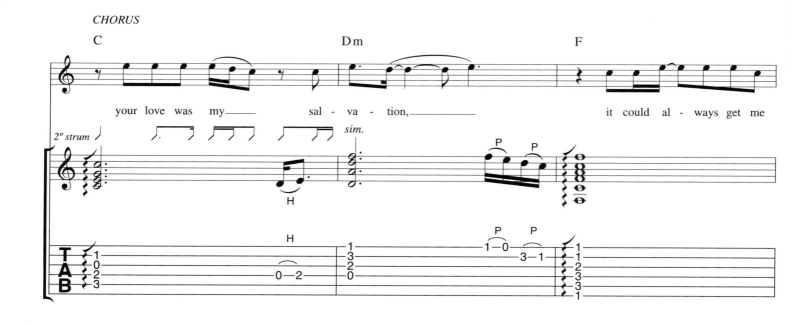

your love was my_____ sal - va - tion,_____ it could al - ways get me

high._____ What was once ho - ly wa - ter_____

1.

tastes like bit - ter wine._____

tastes   like   bit - ter   wine._____

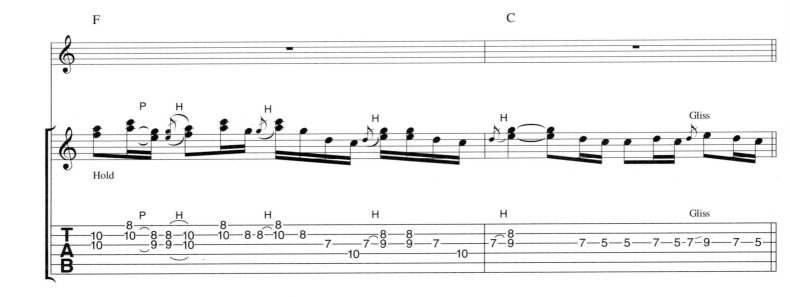

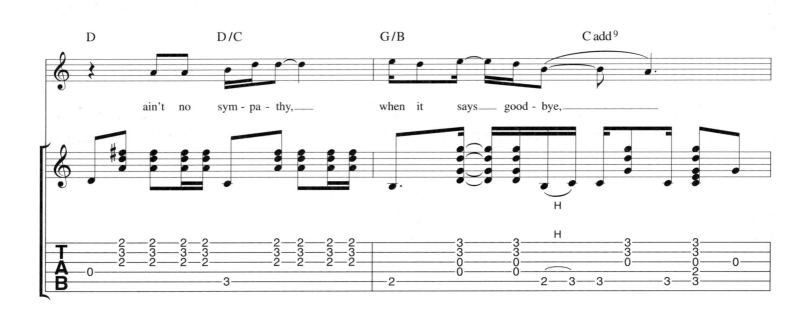

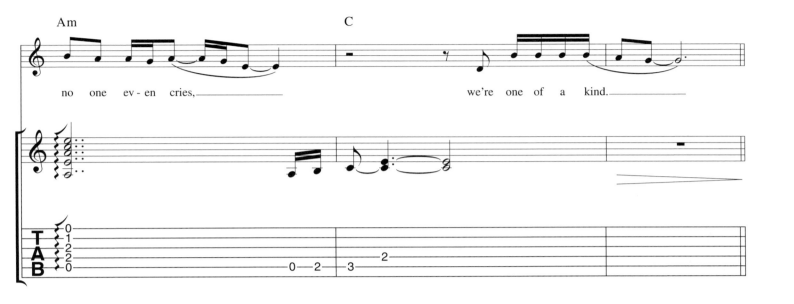

no   one   ev - en   cries,_____   we're   one   of   a   kind._____

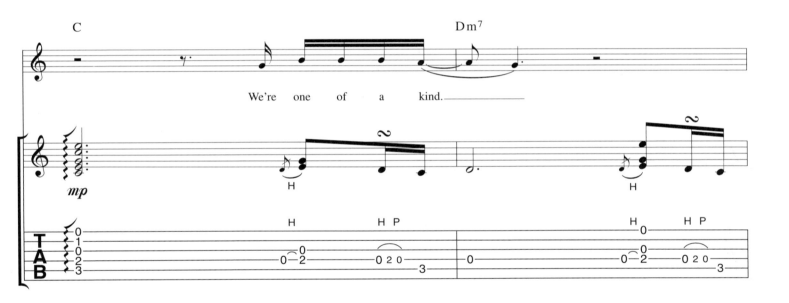

We're   one   of   a   kind._____

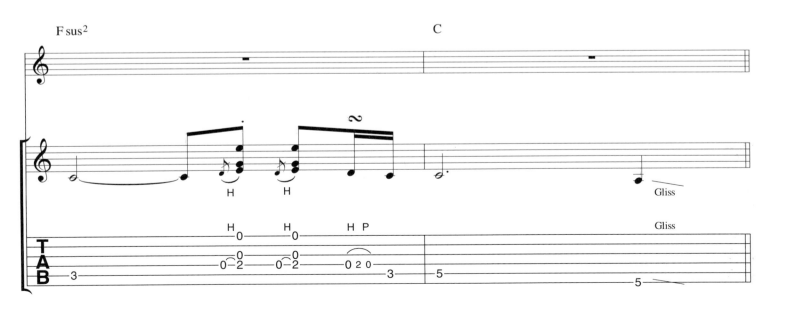

Love left me strand - ed at ____ the sta - tion ____
Your love was my ____ sal - va - tion ____

(2° strum and fills)

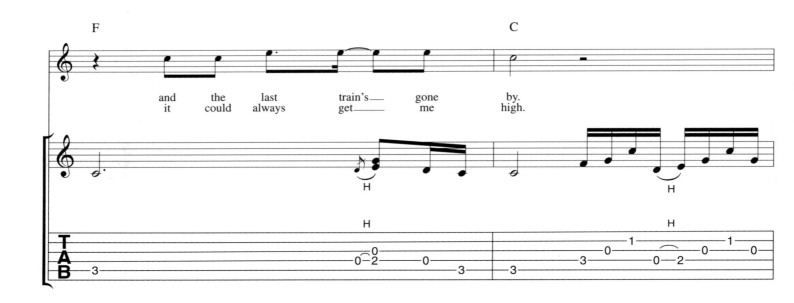

and the last train's ____ gone by.
it could always get ____ me high.

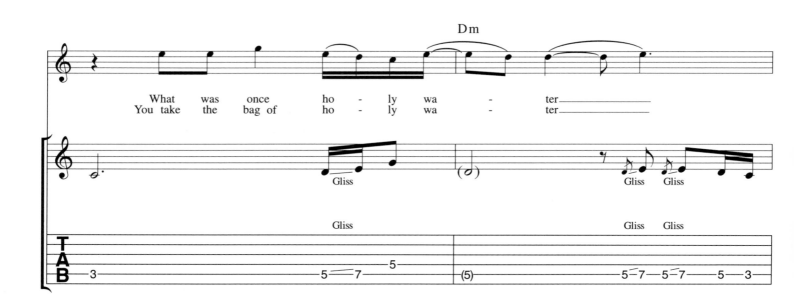

What was once ho - ly wa - ter ____
You take the bag of ho - ly wa - ter ____

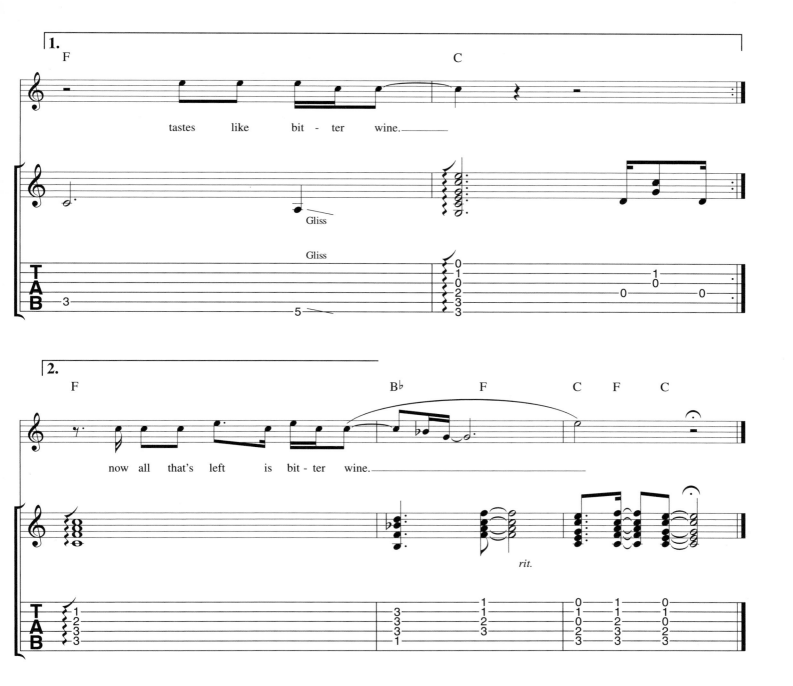

Verse 2:
I know I wasn't funny but you laughed at all my jokes
When I was choking on the words to say you stuck your fingers down my throat
The first night I said I loved you, you told me to go to hell
You were giving me head on that creaky old bed at the ol' Duval motel.

Just like everything, even good love has to die
Ain't no sympathy when it says goodbye.